God-Sized Pages

God-Sized Pages

Floriano Ponte de Melo

RESOURCE *Publications* · Eugene, Oregon

GOD-SIZED PAGES

Resource Publications
An Imprint of Wipf and Stock Publishers
199 W. 8th Ave., Suite 3
Eugene, OR 97401

www.wipfandstock.com

PAPERBACK ISBN: 979-8-3852-5599-3
HARDCOVER ISBN: 979-8-3852-5600-6
EBOOK ISBN: 979-8-3852-5601-3

Introduction

This is not a book. It's a burning structure. One hundred rooms. Each one locked behind your eyelids. You won't agree with them all. You shouldn't. These are not arguments. These are confrontations. Every page is a room you enter alone. Leave something behind in each.

Welcome to the cathedral made of nerves. Welcome to *God-Sized Pages*.

Room 1: The Paper God Bleeds On

God never wrote a word. Men did. While starving, hallucinating, hallucinating about starvation. They called it scripture. We called it truth. God stayed silent.

Ink is not holy. It's just blood trying to behave. Every holy book is a hostage letter written by a soul negotiating with fear.

But let's get precise: the ancient writers were not transmitting divine dictation—they were encoding trauma, ecstasy, the neurological overflow of altered states. Mircea Eliade understood this. William James documented it. When your brain is suffocating from fasting, fear, or fever, it writes scripture.

Scripture is the fossil of the mystical. But we treat it as GPS.

You think words can hold God? Language evolved to warn of predators and woo mates. Not to define eternity. We domesticated sound into symbols, then tried to trap the infinite in a sentence.

The truth? God doesn't speak in words. He speaks in ruptures. Breakdowns. Dead ends. Unexpected grace. A cancer scan. A child's laughter. Grief that bends time. Awe that strips language.

Scripture is what remains after God leaves the room.

These pages are not sacred. They're soaked.

Read with gloves.

Room 2: Heaven Is a Bookstore With No Exit

Imagine an endless bookstore. No staff. No clocks. Every book claims to be the answer. Every page contradicts the next. Some are in tongues you can't even pronounce.

This is heaven for the dead and hell for the thinking.

The shelves go on forever. Nietzsche and Aquinas face off in aisle twelve. Camus whispers in French from the shadows. The self-help section burns constantly but never turns to ash.

You walk in with questions. You leave with questions that can ask better questions. That's progress, if you survive it.

We worship authors but ignore the cost. Writing is surgery without anesthesia. Reading is resurrection with the risk of infection. And belief? That's burial in someone else's casket.

The first sin wasn't eating the fruit. It was quoting God.

Books are seductive. They sell closure like heroin. But behind every sentence is a void, daring you to jump. The universe doesn't speak in conclusions. It stutters in paradox.

Cognitive science tells us we crave coherence more than truth. The brain's default mode network invents narrative just to fill silence. Your favorite book may be a comfort blanket stitched from someone else's delusion.

The Stoics said to read as if you were dying. Sartre said books are a trap. Borges made a library a labyrinth. No one promised you clarity.

You want the truth? It's in the fire alarm you keep ignoring. Every dogma is a book nailed to a door no one opens.

The wise don't escape. They burn the bookstore.

Room 3: Certainty Is a Coffin Lined With Scripture

Certainty is not strength. It's rigor mortis.

The truly alive are in motion—doubt, tension, paradox, suspension. To be certain is to be calcified, to have turned mystery into marble and built a grave.

Look at the history of thought. Certainty has always preceded collapse. Galileo faced a church certain of the cosmos. Hypatia was murdered by men certain of God. Certainty kills before it corrects.

And yet we crave it. Why? Because uncertainty triggers the amygdala. The same primal part of the brain that lights up during threat detection. We feel unsafe not knowing. So we build doctrine, not truth. Safety, not depth.

But faith without doubt is not faith. It's obedience cosplaying as enlightenment.

The best minds knew this. Kierkegaard said faith was a leap into absurdity. Socrates confessed he knew nothing. Buddha refused metaphysical speculation. They were brave enough to stay in the question.

If your beliefs don't make you bleed, you're not believing—you're insulating.

We love quoting dead prophets so we don't have to listen to living questions. Scripture becomes a taxidermy of revelation. Pretty, preserved, and utterly inert.

Jesus didn't write. He was disrupted. He spoke in riddles. He erased lines instead of drawing them. The moment you turn that into a manual, you've already missed the message.

3

Science, at its best, is humility in motion. It does not seek finality. It seeks falsifiability. The second a theory becomes untouchable, it stops being science and becomes religion. And we've got enough religions.

You say you're certain? Then tell me the exact shape of your soul. Define love in atomic terms. Describe death without using metaphor.

You can't. And that's holy.

The coffin is lined with scripture. But the living dig with questions.

Room 4: Grace Is Gravity Wearing a Mask

Grace doesn't arrive with wings. It arrives with bruises.

It is not comfort. It is not ease. It is the moment just after you've destroyed something irreversibly, and yet, still—somehow—you're not destroyed.

Grace is gravity that pulls you from the ledge just as your fingers slip. Not to save you cleanly, but to shatter you safely.

Theologians write poems about grace, but grace isn't poetic. It's the algebra of agony. It's the physics of forgiveness when nothing is fair. It's unjust mercy, undeserved math.

In neuroscience, compassion lights up the same circuits as physical pain. To extend grace is to absorb part of someone else's suffering as your own. That's biology. That's brutal.

And to receive grace? That's worse. Because it means admitting you needed it. That you failed. That you fell. That you couldn't crawl out alone. And the ego would rather burn than bend.

Grace is not the erasure of sin. It's the integration of it. Carl Jung understood this. He called it shadow work. True transformation doesn't come from denial—it comes from absorbing your darkness without being devoured by it.

Religions dress grace in gold, but grace shows up in gutters. It's not sanctified. It's scandalous. It makes no sense. That's why it's real.

You don't ask for grace. It just happens—like falling. You don't catch it. You survive it.

And afterward, you wonder how you're still breathing.

Grace is gravity. But sometimes it wears a mask so you'll stop blaming God for the fall.

Room 5: The Lie That Invented Time

Time is a language we use to explain decay.

We pretend it flows like a river. It doesn't. It's a clock nailed to the skull, measuring guilt. The past isn't behind you. It's inside you—etched in your nervous system, lighting up your amygdala every time memory masquerades as the present.

Einstein shattered our illusions: time is relative, elastic, warped by mass and motion. It is not absolute. It is not fixed. It bends. And if time bends, so does your story.

We say "time heals." No. Time distorts. It makes you forget how deep the wound went. But the scar still knows. Trauma isn't stored in the past. It's stored in the body.

The ancients weren't stupid. They measured life in cycles, not lines. Moons, seasons, recurrences. Only modern minds, enslaved by industrial machinery, believed time should tick forward like a machine gun.

We built calendars like cages and called that progress. But God never invented time. We did—because we couldn't stomach eternity.

Augustine said he knew what time was until someone asked him to explain it. Hawking called it a stubborn illusion. Buddhist monks dismiss it entirely. Only Western minds obsess over being "on schedule."

Time is a theology in disguise. It teaches you to defer being. To sacrifice the present for the mirage of later. To fear death as a deadline instead of seeing it as punctuation.

You are not running out of time. You are running out of stories to tell yourself about who you think you are.

The resurrection isn't about clocks stopping. It's about the narrative collapsing.

You were eternal until someone asked you your birthday.

Room 6: God as the Final Addict

What if God is not the unmoved mover but the most obsessed presence in the cosmos?

Addicted to creation. Addicted to witnessing. Addicted to watching us flail with the free will He handed us like a loaded gun.

Theologians insist on perfection, but perfection doesn't create. Perfection contemplates. Creation is chaotic, messy, desperate—addictive.

Look at the universe. Expansion without end. Galaxies thrown like dice. Black holes swallowing time itself. What kind of mind invents infinity unless it's chasing something it can't reach?

Addiction is repetition with hope. The drunk drinks again. The lover returns to pain. The artist paints another canvas. God creates another world.

And always, the same question: will they choose Me this time?

We're told God is love. But maybe love, in its most obsessive form, is addiction.

In psychological terms, addiction hijacks the dopamine system. It loops desire around lack. Now re-read the Old Testament. The jealous God. The testing. The bargaining. The rage. The reconciliation. That isn't stoic divinity. That's longing that won't die.

And if we're made in His image, isn't our compulsive search for meaning just divine recursion?

Freud would call it neurosis. Jung would say it's individuation. Simone Weil called it hunger for the good. But maybe it's just shared addiction—our creator's and ours, mirroring back and forth like echo chambers made of flesh.

Even the crucifixion—was that salvation or codependence?

The addict always returns. The addict always believes this time, this dose, this prayer, this person, will be enough.

Maybe God keeps creating because He can't stop. Maybe that's what grace really is: the fallout of divine withdrawal.

Room 7: Faith Is a Bridge Over a Fire You Started

Faith is not comfort. It's not belief. It's not certainty dressed in Sunday clothes. Faith is leaping across a chasm with no guarantee the other side exists.

And the twist? You're the one who lit the chasm on fire.

You torched the safe ground behind you with doubt, with questions, with all the heresies you didn't say out loud but lived anyway. You made the bridge necessary by destroying the road.

That's what Kierkegaard meant. The leap of faith isn't heroic. It's desperate. It's the last act of a mind that's exhausted all logic, all reason, all systems—and still refuses nihilism.

In neurological terms, faith doesn't live in the rational prefrontal cortex. It lights up the limbic system—the same regions activated by love, by music, by trauma. Faith isn't thought. It's a survival instinct wrapped in myth.

Think of the child who believes their parents will return, even after ten years of silence. Or the prisoner who imagines sunlight while buried in concrete. That's not theology. That's something deeper.

Faith is your brain saying: "I know none of this makes sense. But let's keep breathing anyway."

Religion tries to institutionalize it. Dogma tries to domesticate it. But raw faith? Real faith? It's feral. It's the scream in the dark when you've forgotten all the words.

The bridge is burning. The fire is yours. But you step anyway.

Because even if you fall, something in you knows: to not leap would be worse.

That's faith.

Room 8: Truth Is a Blade With No Handle

Everyone says they want the truth. But what they really want is confirmation in a prettier font.

Truth isn't handed to you. It's handed through you. And it cuts.

This is why most people run toward comfort dressed as doctrine. Because real truth doesn't cradle. It cleaves. It slices away illusion, pride, identity. It's a blade with no handle—if you try to hold it, it bleeds you.

The Greek word for truth is *aletheia*, which means "uncovering." But what happens when what's uncovered is unbearable?

Science reveals a universe that doesn't care. Evolution is not designed—it is accidental refinement through death. The cosmos expands without purpose. Your body is stardust recycled through meat. There is no script. No safety net. No parents watching.

And still—still—we seek meaning.

Nietzsche understood this. "If you gaze long into the abyss, the abyss gazes also into you." Truth does not arrive gently. It interrogates the one who asks.

In Zen Buddhism, enlightenment comes not through answers, but through *koans*—riddles designed to destroy your logic. Why? Because the truth isn't a solution. It's a reset. A recalibration of everything you thought you knew.

Most religions sell truth with a smile. But the mystics—Meister Eckhart, Rumi, Simone Weil—they spoke of truth as annihilation. Of ego. Of illusion. Of self.

Because the truth doesn't feel good. It feels like grief. Like waking up and realizing everything you believed was a well-decorated lie.

And once you've touched it, there's no going back. Not to doctrine. Not to certainty. Not to sleep.

You carry the blade. No handle. Just the truth. And blood.

Room 9: You Were Not Born. You Were Authored.

Birth is biology. But identity is narrative.

You think you arrived naked into the world, untouched, unwritten. False. You were named. Framed. Filed. Your first cries interpreted through someone else's script. Before you even knew language, you were being programmed by it.

To be human is to be edited.

Your culture handed you plot points: gender, race, religion, nation. Your parents filled in character traits. Your education assigned themes. By the time you said "I," the story had already decided what kind of 'I' you were allowed to be.

Michel Foucault showed how identity is surveillance. You internalize the eye that watches. You play the role you think will be rewarded. Not authenticity—performance.

Neuroscience confirms this: the self is not fixed. It's a construction built from memory, emotion, and external validation. The 'you' you think you are is a flexible fiction written in real time.

And what is trauma but a torn page in your internal narrative—something you can't read, can't integrate, can't skip?

You were not born pure. You were born into a grammar of power. You were not created. You were composed.

The question is: who is holding the pen now?

Most people never ask. They follow the plot laid out for them. But if you stop—really stop—you can feel the edits. You can find the seams. And maybe, just maybe, you can start writing back.

That's the revolt. Not to erase your story. But to revise it.

You weren't born. You were authored. But authors can become editors.

Room 10: When Logic Fails, We Call It Holy

There comes a point where logic runs out of road. And what do we do when that happens? We build a church on the cliff's edge and call the fall divine.

This is not an attack on logic. It is a confession about its limits.

Logic is a closed system. Beautiful, clean, self-referential. But as Gödel proved, no consistent system can prove its own consistency. Translation? Logic always leaves something out.

We fill that void with ritual. With myth. With faith.

Every religion starts with the assumption that something is beyond reason. But then it builds doctrines pretending it isn't. That's the paradox: we use irrationality to touch the infinite, then use rational arguments to defend it.

Mystics knew better. They didn't explain God—they described collapse. Rumi danced. Meister Eckhart vanished into negative theology. Laozi said the Tao that can be named is not the eternal Tao.

Meanwhile, the apologists sharpen syllogisms like spears, trying to defend what by definition cannot be defended—only encountered.

Even science bows here. Quantum mechanics defies intuition. Wave-particle duality laughs at binary thinking. The observer effect makes the act of measurement part of the system. The universe is not logical. It's participatory.

And yet we pretend that reason is the highest form of understanding.

But what if love is more accurate than logic? What if art is truer than argument?

Maybe the things that don't make sense are not flaws—but fingerprints.

When logic fails, we call it holy. Not because we've given up—but because we've finally shut up long enough to listen.

Room 11: Shame—The Original Sacrament

Before the altar, before the blood, before the commandments—there was shame.

It arrived like a second skin in Eden, long before law, long before hell. Adam didn't run because he sinned. He ran because he felt seen.

Shame is older than sin. And far more honest.

Modern psychology backs this. Paul Gilbert, Brené Brown, and Carl Jung all knew: shame is the emotional root system of the human condition. Guilt says, "I did something wrong." Shame says, "I am wrong." It's identity-level. It's bone-deep.

And yet—it's the doorway to transformation.

Religions made shame a tool of control. But the mystics saw it differently. Julian of Norwich called it the first echo of divine awareness. St. Teresa of Ávila bathed in it like it was fire that cleansed rather than consumed.

Shame is the moment you see the mask for what it is. The burning face. The urge to hide. It's what happens when the false self cracks, and for a split second, the soul screams.

In evolutionary terms, shame evolved as social glue. It kept the tribe together. But now it isolates. We drown alone in silence, thinking we're the only ones exiled.

But what if shame is not the enemy? What if it's the invitation?

It strips you down. Not to punish—but to prepare. The ego must die before rebirth is possible. Every sacred transformation begins in ashes, not in glory.

The sacrament was never the wafer or the wine. It was the moment you looked in the mirror and could no longer lie.

Shame is sacred. Not because it's pleasant. But because it tells the truth no sermon dares to say.

Room 12: The Church That Exists Between Two People

It isn't made of bricks. It isn't stained glass and pulpits and creeds. The most dangerous church is the one that forms in the silence between two people who finally tell the truth.

Real connection is sacrament. But it terrifies us. Because in that sacred closeness, there's no place to hide.

Martin Buber called it the "I-Thou" relationship—the sacred spark when one subject truly sees another, not as a thing, but as a soul. In that space, the divine emerges—not imposed, but uncovered.

This is not a church you can build. It's one you become.

In neuroscience, mirror neurons allow us to feel what the other feels. Empathy is not metaphor—it's biology. When you cry and I feel it, that's not poetry. That's synaptic liturgy.

But most of our relationships are temples of defense. Scripts. Roles. Masks. We speak in rehearsed lines and call it intimacy. We perform and call it love.

The real church begins when the performance dies.

Two people, no armor. Two stories, no censorship. One silence, no escape.

No one officiates this kind of union. There's no priest. No choir. No altar. Only risk. Only exposure. And if you're lucky, presence.

Because presence is holy.

Not because it's peaceful—but because it's honest.

This church burns constantly. It does not seek converts. It seeks witnesses.

And once you've stood in its flame, every other ritual feels like ash.

Room 13: Your Body as a Burning Scroll

You are not made of matter. You are made of message.

Every scar, every craving, every tremble in your voice is a syllable written in flesh. Your body is not the vessel of your story. It *is* the story—tattooed in nerve endings, etched in cortisol, encoded in posture and pulse.

The mystics knew it before the doctors did. Teresa of Ávila shook in ecstasy. The Desert Fathers fasted until their bones became scripture. Modern science only caught up centuries later: trauma is not remembered—it is *relived*. The body keeps the score, as van der Kolk said. It remembers everything.

Your jaw holds the secrets you never spoke. Your back carries the expectations you never agreed to. Your stomach digests every threat you couldn't flee.

You call it anxiety. Your body calls it prophecy.

In Jewish tradition, Torah scrolls were sacred because they bore the Name. But what if the divine name is encrypted in your DNA? What if the real scripture is biological? Written in mitochondria. Whispered in hormones. Read aloud in sweat.

We keep looking for revelation in books. But maybe God writes in blood pressure. In grief that breaks your ribs. In orgasms that silence the mind.

You want transcendence? Start by listening to your own tissue.

Because before there was a Word, there was a body. And it burned.

And it still does.

Room 14: The Devil Wrote Psalms Too

Not all beauty is holy. Not all scripture is sacred. Not all inspiration comes from light.

Some of the most haunting verses were written in darkness—by those who understood God too well to worship blindly.

We like to imagine the Devil as the liar. But in Job, it's Satan who speaks honestly. He doesn't tempt Job. He tests the scaffolding of his faith. And God allows it. Sanctions it. Participates in it.

If the Devil exists, he doesn't wear horns. He wears insight. He is the part of you that won't settle for easy answers. The interrogator. The whisperer of *what if*. He doesn't destroy faith—he exposes whether it's hollow.

Dostoevsky knew this. In *The Brothers Karamazov*, Ivan's rebellion against divine justice is more spiritual than the monk's obedience. Ivan wrestles with God like Jacob in the dark. That's the Devil's work—and maybe that's what makes it sacred.

Even Jesus was tempted with scripture. Even scripture can be weaponized.

So what makes a psalm holy? Not the author. Not the ink. Not the tradition that canonized it.

What makes it holy is its capacity to reveal what's real.

Sometimes that revelation comes from saints. Sometimes it comes from serpents.

And if your theology can't handle the Devil quoting truth, then maybe it isn't truth you're after—just comfort.

The Devil wrote psalms too. And some of them still sing.

Room 15: No One Survives Their Own Meaning

We all want to matter. But meaning has a cost.

It begins innocent. You seek purpose. A reason. A thread through chaos. But once found, meaning demands blood. It consumes. It ossifies.

You become its priest. Its pawn. Its prisoner.

Victor Frankl believed meaning could save a man from despair. And it can. But he also warned: when meaning collapses, so does the psyche. Because when your "why" dies, your identity dies with it.

Meaning is not neutral. It organizes everything—memory, desire, fear. And when it becomes too fixed, it fossilizes. Your life becomes a shrine to a sentence you no longer believe.

We don't fear death. We fear dying before our meaning completes. But here's the twist: it never completes.

Camus understood this. He called it absurdity—the gap between our hunger for meaning and the universe's silence. His answer wasn't despair. It was defiance. Live as if meaning exists, knowing it doesn't.

But most can't. So we mythologize ourselves. We turn our jobs into callings. Our pain into plot. Our trauma into teleology. We script our suffering to make it sacred. And then we spend our lives defending that script from edits.

But the self is not a story—it's the author's hand cramping halfway through.

No one survives their own meaning. Because meaning is not a destination. It's the fire you walk through, not the house you build.

Eventually, the story you wrote will burn. And if you're lucky—
you'll walk out alive.

Room 16: Consciousness Is a Cruel Afterthought

We like to believe consciousness is the crown jewel of evolution. That self-awareness is our gift, our superpower. But what if it's a glitch? A cruel afterthought? A side effect of brains that got too good at predicting danger?

You weren't born conscious. You woke into it, slowly. Like surfacing in a room you didn't ask to be in. Then you noticed the mirrors. Then you realized the mirrors were watching back.

Consciousness is the condition of knowing you're temporary—and pretending you're not.

Antonio Damasio, neuroscientist and author, explained that consciousness emerges from layers: the proto-self (basic regulation), the core self (awareness in the moment), and the autobiographical self (your story). But that story isn't real. It's retrofitted. Post-facto.

Your brain invents continuity. You didn't live a life—you remembered it into existence.

Even your choices may be illusions. Libet's experiments in the 1980s revealed that the brain makes decisions milliseconds before "you" become aware of them. Free will may be the narrative the brain tells to rationalize what's already been done.

You are not the driver. You are the commentator.

And yet—we build ethics, empires, religions atop this flickering fiction. We cry when a character dies in a movie, and forget that our "self" is a character too. Worse, it knows it.

Other animals live. Humans witness.

We are ghosts who haven't died yet. Consciousness is the haunting. A flashlight in a dark hallway that can't shut off—and shows you everything you didn't want to see.

So we build distractions. We worship ignorance. We sedate. We scroll.

Because if you stare too long at the fact that you are watching yourself, you begin to realize:

There is no escape from the mirror. Only different rooms to reflect in.

Room 17: Salvation by Sabotage

You will not be saved by trying harder.

Salvation does not come through polishing the mask. It comes when the mask cracks under pressure you thought you couldn't survive—and didn't. At least, not the version of you that wore it.

We've been taught that salvation is a ladder. You climb toward light, obedience, purity, perfection. But what if it's not? What if salvation is the moment you fall off the ladder and realize there was never anything above you—just the ground waiting to hold you?

You don't ascend into truth. You collapse into it.

In psychological terms, ego dissolution is not death—it's breakthrough. Carl Jung said, "One does not become enlightened by imagining figures of light, but by making the darkness conscious." The path forward is a descent. Downward. Inward. Into shadow.

Real healing begins when the persona—the curated self—fails. The marriage fails. The belief system fails. The reputation fails. These are not punishments. These are permissions. To finally rebuild something honest.

The theology of self-improvement is a trap. It weaponizes grace into performance. It turns spirituality into another addiction—chasing worthiness.

But grace, when it's real, is not earned. It's endured.

Sabotage is usually seen as failure. But sometimes it's the unconscious saying "no more." It's the divine veto. The internal insurgency that destroys the false altar so something raw and real can emerge.

Your salvation might not look like healing. It might look like divorce. Like bankruptcy. Like silence. Like walking away.

It might look like destruction. Because that's what it takes to unmake the lie you've mistaken for a life.

Sabotage is not the opposite of salvation. Sometimes, it's how it begins.

Room 18: When Prayer Becomes Plagiarism

Prayer was never meant to be recited. It was meant to be wrestled.

But most of us don't pray. We mimic. We quote. We recycle someone else's yearning in hopes it'll count for ours. We plagiarize emotion, outsource intimacy, and call it devotion.

That's not prayer. That's a performance.

True prayer is not polite. It is not rhythmic. It does not rhyme. It breaks form. It breaks you. It's the scream that doesn't fit in a liturgy, the silence that no scripture can fill.

Abraham argued. Jacob limped. Job accused. Jesus wept and bled and begged. Not one of them sounded like a choir.

Real prayer is unpublishable.

But religion teaches us scripts. Formulas. Templates. It sanitizes desperation into doctrine. It replaces ache with aesthetics. And in doing so, it steals the sacred tension between soul and source.

In neuroscience, the default mode network is where we self-reflect. It activates during unstructured, inward focus—like prayer. But rote recitation bypasses this system. You're not connecting. You're repeating. Autopilot spirituality.

The Psalms worked not because they were poetic, but because they were raw. Rage, betrayal, longing, lust, confusion. They weren't written to impress. They were written to survive.

So ask yourself: if your prayer was recorded and played back, would it sound like a man on fire—or a man reading a weather report?

If God is listening, why do you sound like you're talking to a board meeting?

Prayer that doesn't cost you something isn't prayer. It's plagiarism.

The soul's real language doesn't have grammar. It has gravity.

Room 19: The Soul's Suicide Note

Every person you meet is a slow-motion collapse. Smiling. Functioning. Posting. Dying.

The soul doesn't scream. It whispers—so softly you need silence to hear it. But silence terrifies us. So we fill it with noise, distraction, theology, ambition, routine. We stay busy so we don't have to read what's been written inside.

Because deep down, many have already quit.

They haven't ended their lives. They've just stopped living them.

They stay in the marriage but never touch. They show up to work but haven't dreamed in a decade. They bow their heads in prayer but haven't believed in years.

This is the soul's suicide: slow, civil, socially acceptable.

You can't measure it in blood, but you can see it in posture. In eyes that have turned into windows no longer cleaned. In laughter that doesn't rise from the gut. In art that used to be sacred, now shelved.

The existentialists weren't pessimists. They were honest. Kierkegaard called it despair—the sickness unto death. Camus called it absurdity. A silent war between meaning and meaninglessness.

And Freud? He called it Thanatos—the death drive. A pull toward unbeing that fights the urge to persist.

But here's the secret: the soul doesn't want to die. It wants to be seen.

Every suicide note is a love letter written to silence: "Please, notice me before I disappear."

Your soul has probably been writing drafts for years. Every time you lied to protect an image. Every time you said "I'm fine" when you were breaking. Every time you stopped creating because it wouldn't be perfect.

This is not about dying. This is about waking up before you do.

Burn the suicide note. Write a resurrection instead.

Room 20: The Architect Is Also the Ruin

We want to believe the builder is separate from the wreckage. That the creator floats above collapse. That the hands that designed the temple are not the same hands that dropped the match.

But every architect leaves fingerprints in the rubble.

The God who breathes life also breathes storms. The parent who raises you also warps you. The mind that dreamed your ideals also sabotaged them. The self that reached for transcendence also swallowed poison.

Creation and destruction are not opposites. They are twin compulsions—inseparable, interdependent. Nietzsche called it eternal recurrence. The wheel doesn't just spin—it grinds.

In physics, entropy is law. Every structure tends toward disorder. And if you think souls are exempt, you haven't been paying attention.

The house you built out of belief will eventually sink under the weight of your questions. The foundation will crack. The roof will leak. And one day, you'll realize you are living inside your own metaphor—one you can't maintain.

And still, you build.

Because ruin is not the end. Ruin is the unveiling. It reveals what can't be destroyed.

The architect isn't innocent. But neither is he finished.

Every collapse is a blueprint—drawn in reverse. Every failure is a revision. Every ruin is still holy ground.

Because the God who writes the story is also written by it. And maybe that's the real divinity: Not omnipotence. But participation.

Room 21: Angels Don't Carry Answers

Every time they show up in scripture, the first thing angels say is: "Do not be afraid."

Which means you should be.

Because when heaven speaks, it doesn't bring clarity. It brings rupture. Divine messengers are not therapists. They're shockwaves. They don't hand you peace. They hand you a decision so heavy it shatters who you were before they arrived.

Gabriel didn't explain. He announced. A sword to Mary's expectations. A detonation to Joseph's plans. And what was the response? Not certainty. Not confidence. Just obedience wrapped in dread.

We keep asking for signs. We forget signs destroy maps.

Angels are not cute. They're not safe. Ezekiel saw beings with wheels inside wheels, eyes in every direction. Isaiah's vision burned his mouth. John fell as though dead.

These aren't symbols of comfort. They are embodiments of disruption.

Carl Jung wrote that the encounter with the Self—the true, undivided psyche—is both sacred and terrifying. An angel is not a metaphor for goodness. It's a mirror you can't lie to.

Angels don't carry answers. They carry announcements. Change. Collapse. Conception.

You don't get to ask questions. You get to respond—or refuse.

And maybe the reason you haven't heard from heaven is because you're still pretending you'd say yes.

Room 22: Prophets Speak in Past Tense

We think prophets predict the future. But real prophets don't forecast—they *remember*.

They speak not from visions, but from wounds. From exile. From the jagged edge of what already happened while the rest of us were too comfortable to notice.

Prophecy isn't magic. It's clarity sharpened by suffering.

Amos didn't charm kings. Jeremiah wept in public. Elijah hid in caves. These men weren't seers—they were mirrors. And we smashed them because we didn't like the reflection.

We ask for prophets but want politicians. Charisma over confrontation. Echoes over honesty.

But the real ones are inconvenient. Angry. Bleeding. They come from the margins and speak in metaphors too raw for TED Talks.

In social psychology, the majority resists dissent until reality makes it unbearable. Prophets are society's immune response—overactive, hypersensitive, and always early. We call them crazy until we need them. Then we call them dead.

Walter Brueggemann said that prophets reframe reality. They don't argue. They disrupt. They destabilize the dominant imagination until something new can be seen.

Prophets don't offer answers. They burn the script. They say, "You already know."

You just haven't admitted it yet.

That's why they speak in past tense. Because by the time a true prophet finishes speaking, it's already too late.

Room 23: Holiness Is What You Do With Your Damage

Holiness isn't purity. It's not performance, or posture, or pretending you've never bled.

Holiness is what you build from the wreckage. It's what you choose to carry and what you choose to set down. It's the art of transmuting pain into presence.

Religions often mistake cleanliness for sanctity. But the sacred has always emerged from what we try to hide: lepers, beggars, tax collectors, whores. Jesus didn't avoid contamination—he embodied it, then rewrote what it meant.

Modern therapy echoes ancient mysticism: the wound is the portal. Carl Jung said, "Only the wounded physician heals." Gabor Maté writes that trauma isn't what happens to you, but what happens inside you. Holiness begins when you stop denying either.

Real sanctity is scarred. It doesn't quote scripture—it survives it.

You want to see holiness? Look at the addict who chooses day one again. The parent who stays present after the apology. The artist who paints with trembling hands. The man who still prays after the miracle didn't come.

You were told to erase your damage to be holy. But the holiest ones are the ones who let it speak. Who let it guide. Who let it shape a truth that doesn't need to be pretty to be powerful.

God doesn't need your perfection. He wants your participation.

Your damage is not your disqualification. It's your invitation.

Room 24: Mercy Has No Memory

We assume mercy keeps score. That forgiveness is a courtroom transaction, a ledger wiped clean, a moral bookkeeping miracle.

But mercy isn't mathematical. It forgets on purpose.

Not because it's naive, but because it knows remembering too well is another form of punishment.

In most human systems, justice requires memory. The law remembers. Prisons remember. Your family remembers. You remember. But mercy is not interested in what happened. It's obsessed with what *could* happen if the past weren't always dragging behind.

In trauma studies, the nervous system replays pain like a broken record. Mercy is the hand that lifts the needle.

It's not amnesia. It's alchemy.

Mercy says: *you are more than the worst thing you've done.* And more than the worst thing done to you. And more than the version of yourself you keep resuscitating just so you can punish it again.

That kind of forgetting isn't a flaw. It's divine strategy.

In the Christian scriptures, God says He will remember sin no more. Not that He'll erase it. But that He'll choose not to recall it. Mercy isn't ignorance. It's resistance.

You want to be merciful? Then forget the version of that person who hurt you—so they have a chance to become someone else.

You want to receive mercy? Then stop dragging your corpse into every conversation.

Mercy is not a second chance. It's the refusal to count.

Because love keeps no record of wrongs. And mercy burns the ledger.

Room 25: Heaven Has a Back Door

No one gets into heaven clean.

We've been sold a front entrance—guarded by doctrine, polished by behavior, earned by discipline. But the front door was built for the perfect, and perfection is a myth engineered to keep you outside.

The real way in is through the back.

Through the cracks. Through the grief that unmakes you. Through the mercy that didn't make sense. Through the addiction that taught you honesty. Through the breakdown that rewired your soul.

All the sacred ones stumbled in sideways.

The thief didn't pray. He just confessed. The tax collector beat his chest and couldn't lift his eyes. The woman with seven demons didn't get healed in a synagogue. And Jesus—He broke the locks Himself.

Heaven doesn't take applications. It receives collapse.

It doesn't ask for credentials. It looks for surrender.

In Eastern Orthodox theology, salvation is *theosis*—becoming like God. Not by ascending, but by emptying. Kenosis. Self-pouring. You don't rise. You pour out. That's how you fit through the narrow way.

You want heaven? Start with the back door. The one behind the shame. The one behind the honesty you've never dared to speak. The one behind the forgiveness you still refuse to offer.

Heaven is not a prize. It's a place only the undone can enter.

The back door's always open. But it only opens inward.

Room 26: Worship Is What You Do With Your Wounds

Worship was never about music. It's not the tempo, the chord progression, or the emotional swell. It's what you do with your pain when no one's looking.

True worship starts in the wound. In the place that still bleeds. In the ache that hasn't resolved. It's not praise—it's surrender.

In Hebrew, the word for worship is *shachah*—to bow down, to prostrate. To fall flat. Not in reverence, but in collapse. Worship begins where your strength ends.

David danced in disgrace. Hannah cried so hard they thought she was drunk. Jesus sweat blood. None of it was sanitized. None of it would make it on a modern stage.

Worship is not performance. It's exposure. It's the moment you stop pretending your soul is presentable.

Neuroscience confirms: music activates the limbic system—emotion, memory, instinct. But trauma survivors often experience dissociation during worship. Why? Because music can bypass language. And sometimes, that's too much truth too fast.

We have turned worship into spectacle, but the Spirit still lives in shadows. In caves. In bedrooms. In prisons. In panic attacks and whispered prayers and voices that break halfway through the sentence.

You want to worship? Bring what hurts. Not what's healed.

God doesn't need your harmony. He wants your honesty.

And if your voice cracks, if your hands shake, if your theology breaks in the middle of the chorus—

that's worship too.

Room 27: God Doesn't Speak English

We assume the divine speaks our language. That revelation arrives in grammar. That holiness wears punctuation. That heaven can be translated.

But God doesn't speak English. Or Greek. Or Hebrew. Or Latin. Those are our tongues—our scaffolds. God speaks in flame. In silence. In paradox.

Language is the best we've got—and still not enough. Every word is a cage. Every sentence a compromise. We speak in symbols and assume we're getting truth, when all we've caught is the shadow.

Wittgenstein said, "The limits of my language mean the limits of my world." But we made God a character in our syntax, forgetting that the infinite doesn't bend to nouns.

Mystics across traditions say the same thing: the closer you get to the divine, the less there is to say. The more you stammer. The more you contradict yourself. Because God doesn't sit in clarity. God lives in the rupture.

Language flattens. God explodes.

Even the Bible disagrees with itself—deliberately. Poets contradict historians. Prophets disobey kings. Jesus refuses definitions. Paul reinterprets everything. And still we try to systematize mystery.

You want to hear God? Stop quoting Him. Stop polishing sentences. Stop insisting He fits your dialect.

Go to the place beneath language—where music begins, where dreams fumble, where silence finally gets a word in.

God speaks. But not in English.

Room 28: Holiness Doesn't Happen in Public

We've mistaken visibility for virtue. We perform piety like it's theater. We livestream devotion. We Instagram sacrifice. We treat holiness like a résumé—a record of curated goodness for spiritual approval.

But real holiness doesn't happen in public. It happens in the unlit places. In the privacy of decisions no one will see. In the interior spaces where character is forged, not posted.

Jesus knew this. That's why He said to pray in secret. To fast without announcement. To give without trumpets. Because the sacred isn't spectacle. It's surrender.

In psychology, this is the difference between intrinsic and extrinsic motivation. The truly moral act isn't done for reward or recognition. It's done because it's who you are when no one is watching.

Public piety is easy. It's rehearsed. It's rewarded. But secret integrity? That's dangerous. That's where you face the unfiltered self. That's where the mask doesn't fit.

Holiness doesn't shine. It flickers. It falters. It bleeds.

The holiest people aren't the loudest. They're the ones who carry their pain quietly, who forgive without announcement, who resist the urge to perform righteousness like a sales pitch.

You want to be holy? Turn off the camera. Delete the caption. Let God be the only witness.

Because if your holiness needs an audience, it isn't holiness.

It's branding.

Room 29: Theology Is a House Built After the Fire

No one writes theology in the middle of the blaze. They write it after the ashes settle. After the screaming stops. After the body count is tallied and the soul starts asking, "What just happened?"

Theology is not the voice of God. It's the echo we name after surviving the silence.

Most doctrines are post-trauma architecture. We lost something. We broke. We bled. So we built systems to make sense of it. To scaffold pain into meaning. To turn collapse into curriculum.

But every theological system leaks. Every creed has a crack. Because no human language can perfectly bind a divine explosion.

Karl Barth said all theology is human speech about God's speech. Which means it's already secondhand. At best, we're writing commentary on a language we barely understand.

And yet we weaponize it. We take these post-fire blueprints and use them to judge those still burning.

But theology is meant to be scaffold, not cage. A space to build within—not a box to trap the infinite.

Your ideas about God will evolve. They must. Because you will suffer. Because you will encounter contradiction. Because the God who was safe in your twenties will not survive your thirties unless He changes, or you do.

God doesn't fear your revisions. He's already rewriting you.

Theology isn't truth. It's our best attempt to point at it.

And every time we think we've built something eternal, God moves the fire.

Room 30: Hell Is Just a Room With No Windows

Forget the flames. Forget the pitchforks and devils and boiling pits. Those are distractions—cartoons made by people too afraid to describe the real thing.

Hell isn't a furnace. It's a room where you can't see out.

No sky. No horizon. No connection. Just echo. Just repetition. Just yourself, on loop, forever.

C.S. Lewis came close when he wrote *The Great Divorce*. Hell as a place people choose, not because they love pain—but because they hate surrender. Because they'd rather be right than free.

Psychology agrees. Isolation doesn't just hurt—it dismantles. The brain is wired for connection. Solitary confinement reshapes neural pathways. Hell isn't punishment. It's disintegration.

Dante imagined levels. But the real descent is internal. It's not downward. It's inward.

Every grudge you won't drop. Every lie you keep defending. Every refusal to apologize, to forgive, to soften. These are bricks. You lay them. You mortar them with pride. And eventually, there's no way out.

No devil required. Just you. And a door you locked long ago.

If heaven is union, hell is self-curated exile.

And the longer you stay in the room, the more you forget there was ever a window at all.

Room 31: The Cross Is Not a Symbol

We've turned it into jewelry. Decoration. A logo. We've sanitized the most brutal form of execution ever devised into a brand.

But the cross is not a symbol. It's a crime scene.

The cross is state violence, religious complicity, and divine silence all colliding in a single scream. It's not just where God died—it's where humanity was exposed. It's not a metaphor. It's a mirror.

You don't wear a cross. You carry it. And it's heavy.

Historically, crucifixion was reserved for the most humiliating deaths. Stripped. Nailed. Displayed. Roman terror marketing at its peak. And yet—this is what Jesus chose as the axis of transformation.

Not a throne. Not a temple. A torture device.

Theologian Jürgen Moltmann called it "the crucified God." A deity who doesn't just watch suffering but absorbs it. Participates in it. Becomes indistinguishable from it.

That should terrify us. Because it means there's no spiritual escape hatch. No divine exemption clause. There is no resurrection without rupture.

The cross is not about guilt. It's about gravity. The weight of existence. The pull of pain. The certainty of death.

But it's also about resistance. The refusal to return violence with violence. The declaration that even in agony, love speaks last.

So don't wear the cross until you've stood under it. Until you've felt its silence. Until you've asked why no miracle came.

And still whispered: "I'm not leaving."

Room 32: The Kingdom Is Always Upside Down

Everything we think we know about power—God flips it.

The first are last. The meek inherit. The poor are blessed. The peacemakers are honored. The mourners get the kingdom. It's not just reversal. It's subversion.

The kingdom isn't an empire. It's a wound turned inside out.

We keep trying to build upward—bigger, better, higher. But Jesus digs downward. Toward tables, not thrones. Toward feet, not crowns. Toward sinners, not saints.

Power in the kingdom isn't command. It's compassion. Influence isn't dominance. It's presence. And glory isn't elevation. It's incarnation.

The disciples didn't get it. We still don't. We keep asking for seats of honor. We keep weaponizing theology to prop up patriarchy, supremacy, certainty.

But every time we think we've built a fortress, God plants a garden underneath it.

Theologian James Cone said that any theology not grounded in the suffering of the oppressed is not Christian theology. Because the gospel doesn't just comfort the broken. It breaks the comfortable.

The kingdom doesn't work like the world. It undoes it.

It doesn't climb ladders. It kicks them over.

You want to find the kingdom? Look beneath you. Where you stepped last. Where you looked past. Where you thought God couldn't possibly be.

He's there. Always there. Flipping everything you thought was right-side up.

Room 33: Miracles Are Messy

We want miracles to be clean. Bright lights. Happy endings. Applause.

But real miracles don't tidy things up. They wreck the order you were surviving in.

The bleeding woman interrupted a procession. The man lowered through the roof broke the ceiling. The resurrection blew open a tomb and terrified everyone. Miracles, when real, don't comfort. They confront.

They mess with your schedule, your ego, your theology.

We've sanitized the supernatural into something respectable. Marketable. But scripture never does that. In the Bible, miracles almost always disrupt. People are confused, afraid, rebuked. Jesus heals a man and tells him not to speak of it—because miracles aren't proofs. They're portals.

In modern psychology, change rarely comes through insight alone. It comes through rupture. Through disorientation. That's what a miracle is: psychological and spiritual dislocation that rewrites what you thought was possible.

But most of us don't want that. We want relief, not rebirth.

We want the waters parted, but not the wilderness afterward. We want the healing, not the humility. The deliverance, not the disruption.

And so, when miracles do happen, we often miss them. Because they don't look like magic. They look like breakdowns.

You lose your job—and find your calling. You get rejected—and meet your real self. You grieve—and grow a second heart.

Miracles are messy. Not because God is disordered. But because resurrection always ruins the grave.

Room 34: Prayer Doesn't Work

Not the way you think.

Prayer isn't a cosmic vending machine. It's not input-output. You don't insert desperation and wait for delivery. Prayer isn't transactional. It's confrontational.

It doesn't fix things. It changes who's doing the asking.

The mistake is thinking prayer manipulates God. The truth is prayer dismantles *you*. Your wants. Your illusions. Your control. You kneel thinking you're speaking upward—and find you've opened a trapdoor beneath yourself.

If prayer worked the way we were told, Jesus wouldn't have said "take this cup" and then drunk it anyway.

Real prayer is where theology dies. Where the mask of certainty melts. Where your voice breaks halfway through the sentence and you keep going, not because you believe, but because you have nothing else left.

In neurobiology, the act of prayer activates the same regions of the brain associated with empathy, self-awareness, and surrender. That's not weakness. That's rewiring. That's your nervous system confessing it can't save itself.

Sometimes prayer gets answered. Sometimes it gets echoed. Sometimes it gets buried.

But the point was never the outcome. The point was the rupture. The intimacy. The hollowing out of ego so something divine could echo inside.

Prayer doesn't work. It undoes. And that's the miracle.

Room 35: You Can't Heal Where You Lied

Healing isn't magic. It's alignment.

And you cannot align with what's real while still maintaining what's false.

You can't heal in the same room where you convinced yourself nothing happened. You can't mend in the house you built out of denial. You can't walk free while holding onto the script that kept you safe—but sick.

Every lie costs something. And the cost is connection. To your body. To your truth. To others. To God.

In trauma therapy, one of the first principles is safety. But safety doesn't mean comfort. It means honesty without threat. And as long as you lie—to yourself, to your therapist, to your Creator—you stay fractured.

The limbic system doesn't care about your theology. It stores what's real. It keeps the secrets you keep forgetting. It holds the panic, the pause, the flinch. It won't release until you stop pretending.

Confession isn't for forgiveness. It's for alignment. It's for reality. You say the truth aloud not because God needs to hear it—but because *you* do.

You can't heal what you won't name. You can't name what you've justified.

And until you burn the mask, there's no balm that can touch your skin.

Healing waits. But it won't enter a room still decorated with the lie.

Room 36: Revelation Always Ruins Something

We talk about revelation like it's a gift. A lightbulb. A breakthrough. A divine download.

But real revelation doesn't clarify—it disrupts. It ruins your scaffolding.

It calls you out of the tent you built for safety and shows you the stars—and the terrifying vastness they shine in. It rips the veil and dares you to stare directly at what you spent your whole life avoiding.

When Isaiah saw the Lord, he didn't cheer. He said, "Woe is me." Because to see truth is to see yourself without the costume.

Revelation doesn't make things easier. It makes them undeniable.

You thought you were managing your anger—until the pattern revealed itself. You thought your faith was intact—until silence exposed its scaffolding. You thought your love was pure—until the mirror shattered and showed the control behind the kindness.

In neuroscience, insight rewires the brain. But that rewiring doesn't feel peaceful. It feels like loss. The neurons you've relied on for decades suddenly find themselves obsolete. That's not epiphany. That's ego death.

And yet we crave it. Because even if it wrecks us, it frees us.

God never reveals to impress. He reveals to unmake.

And if you walk away from revelation feeling more comfortable than before—you probably weren't looking at God.

Room 37: You Don't Get to Skip the Wilderness

The wilderness is not a punishment. It's a passage.

Every sacred story walks through it. Every honest soul stumbles into it. And no matter how well you pray, fast, or behave—you don't get to skip it.

The wilderness is where your formulas go to die. Where your theology runs out of breath. Where the voice of God goes quiet—not to torture you, but to teach you how to listen without needing to hear.

You'll try to go back. To Egypt. To comfort. To the gods who at least answered with fire. But there's no map for this terrain. Just dust. Delay. And the ache of what no longer fits.

In trauma psychology, disorientation is the beginning of healing. Not clarity. Disorientation. The wilderness strips your coping mechanisms like dead skin. It's not cruel. It's precise.

Even Jesus was led there—not by sin, but by the Spirit. Not to be pampered, but to be undone.

The wilderness doesn't fix you. It reveals what still breaks you. And it waits. Patient. Relentless. Holy.

No one survives it unchanged. That's the point.

You want resurrection? You have to pass through the desert first. Not around. Through.

Because what's sacred isn't what gets you out of the wilderness.

What's sacred is what refuses to leave you in it.

Room 38: Doubt Is a Type of Devotion

We've demonized doubt. Labeled it weakness. Treated it like a virus that infects faith. But doubt isn't the opposite of belief—it's its refinement.

Blind belief requires nothing. But real faith is forged in friction.

Thomas wasn't punished for doubting. He was invited to touch the wounds. And what did Jesus say? Not "believe harder." He said, "Blessed are those who have not seen." Doubt wasn't condemned. It was dignified.

In spiritual development, doubt is not regression—it's evolution. James Fowler's stages of faith show that questioning is a necessary part of maturity. Stage four is often a collapse of inherited belief. Stage five is where complexity is integrated. Without doubt, you never reach depth.

Philosophers like Kierkegaard embraced doubt as sacred tension. He didn't solve it. He lived in it. Because doubt is what keeps faith from becoming idolatry.

Certainty closes doors. Doubt opens them.

You doubt because you care. You doubt because the questions matter. You doubt because you refuse to fake it.

That's not failure. That's devotion without a mask.

Doubt is not spiritual treason. It's theological honesty.

And if your God can't survive your questions, then your God was never God.

Room 39: Grace Doesn't Care If You Deserve It

We've turned grace into a prize. Something you earn by saying the right things, wearing the right clothes, checking the right boxes. But grace doesn't care about your résumé.

It shows up where it shouldn't. In the stories you'd rather not tell. In the places you pretend you've never been.

Grace is the uninvited guest that breaks into your shame and eats with you anyway.

Jesus didn't offer grace to the polished. He offered it to the excluded, the filthy, the disqualified. Not after they changed—before. Not because they proved themselves—but because they couldn't.

And still we insist on earning it. We turn grace into a transaction. But grace is allergic to contracts. It refuses to be leveraged. You don't summon it. You survive it.

In psychological terms, the experience of unearned kindness rewires the brain. It breaks cycles of shame. It creates space for vulnerability. Grace is not sentiment. It's neurological subversion.

The addict doesn't deserve another chance. But grace gives it. The liar doesn't deserve trust. But grace risks it. The cynic doesn't deserve wonder. But grace keeps showing up anyway.

Deserving was never the metric. Only desperation. Only surrender. Only the moment you stop performing and finally let yourself be seen.

Grace doesn't care if you deserve it. It cares if you'll receive it.

Room 40: The Gospel Is Not Good News for Everyone

Not if you're invested in keeping power. Not if your comfort depends on someone else's silence. Not if your religion props up the system that crucified the messenger.

The gospel—*the real one*—doesn't reassure the empire. It threatens it.

When Jesus said the first would be last, He wasn't being poetic. He was being political. When He flipped tables, He wasn't having a moment. He was making a statement: *This whole thing is upside down.*

We've edited the gospel into something polite. Something marketable. A brand. A slogan. But the real gospel is dangerous. It got people killed. It still does.

Because it doesn't just save. It upends.

It doesn't just comfort. It convicts.

It's not good news to Pharaoh. It's good news to the slaves.

It's not good news to Caesar. It's good news to the crucified.

And if your version of the gospel doesn't make the powerful nervous, it might not be the gospel.

Theologian Gustavo Gutiérrez called it liberation. James Cone called it Black. Dorothy Day called it a revolution disguised as grace.

The gospel is not good news for everyone. It never was. It was good news for the ones everyone else decided didn't matter.

If that offends you, then you're exactly who it came to confront.

Room 41: Sin Is Smaller Than You Think

We've inflated sin into something abstract, systemic, distant. A cosmic legal infraction. But real sin isn't grand. It's subtle. It's ordinary. It's the way you avoid eye contact. It's the sarcasm that hides the wound. It's the silence that lets injustice live longer.

Sin is smaller than you think. And that's what makes it dangerous.

We want sin to be scandal. Something big. Something *they* do. But it's mostly the tiny, repeated choices to devalue what is sacred— starting with ourselves.

The Hebrew word for sin, *chata*, means "to miss the mark." Not to destroy the target. Just to miss. By an inch. A little more each time. And eventually, you're nowhere near who you were meant to be.

It's not just about breaking rules. It's about breaking relationship.

James Baldwin said, "People pay for what they do... and still more for what they have allowed themselves to become." That's sin. The slow shaping of the soul away from truth.

In neuroscience, pathways get strengthened by repetition. Sin is neuroplastic. You become what you repeatedly choose. And when that choice is comfort over courage, numbness over truth, apathy over action—you drift.

Not into evil. But into absence.

Sin doesn't always look like violence. Sometimes it just looks like disengagement.

And repentance? It's not guilt. It's reorientation. It's waking up.

Because the biggest sins aren't what you did. They're what you stopped noticing.

Room 42: Sacred Doesn't Mean Safe

We've confused sacred with soft. We've made the holy into something gentle, pristine, digestible. But sacred things aren't safe—they're seismic.

Every real encounter with the sacred in scripture starts with fear. Moses hid his face. Isaiah cursed himself. Peter begged Jesus to leave. Because holiness is heavy.

It doesn't flatter you. It confronts you.

The sacred doesn't coddle. It calls. And the call always costs something. Comfort. Identity. Certainty. Your grip on the way things were.

The burning bush was sacred, but it wrecked Moses's peace. The tabernacle was sacred, but it killed those who entered unclean. Jesus was sacred—but His presence unraveled the status quo, exposed the frauds, flipped the tables.

In evolutionary psychology, threat perception is tied to survival. When something disrupts our equilibrium, the brain sounds an alarm. The sacred does this—because it demands transformation.

And transformation always feels like danger.

That's why the sacred will never be safe. Because it doesn't leave you where it found you.

You want safety? Find a religion that fits your preferences. You want the sacred? Prepare to be undone.

Because sacred ground is where illusions die. And the only thing left standing—is what was always real.

Room 43: You Can't Unknow What Saved You

Once grace finds you, you're ruined for normal.

You can't go back to pretending. You can't unsee the mercy. You can't unknow the weight that lifted when you had no words and no faith and no reason—and still, somehow, you weren't abandoned.

That's the terrifying thing about real transformation. It doesn't leave quietly.

We romanticize salvation like it's a one-time event. A clean slate. A line in the sand. But the truth? It's a haunting. It follows you. It whispers through your cynicism. It hums behind your arguments. It sits in the quiet after the noise dies down.

Real grace doesn't make you more religious. It makes you more honest.

In psychology, trauma embeds itself into memory networks—it changes how the brain stores reality. But so does awe. So does rescue. The miracle rewires your schema.

You can't unbelong after you've been embraced. You can't return to the lie once you've been kissed by the truth.

You may run. You may deny. You may dress it up as coincidence.

But deep down, beneath the sarcasm and the smirk, you remember the moment the light broke through. And no matter how much you pretend to forget—it's there.

You can't unknow what saved you. You can only decide what you'll do with the memory.

Room 44: Holiness Isn't a Mood

You don't feel your way into holiness. You act your way into it.

We keep waiting to feel spiritual, to feel moved, to feel ready. But holiness doesn't depend on how the moment feels—it depends on what the moment *asks of you*, and whether or not you show up.

It's not about emotional elevation. It's about fidelity in obscurity.

Abraham walked without direction. Ruth stayed without reward. Jeremiah wept without results. None of them felt holy. They just kept saying yes.

We've turned holiness into a vibe—lights, music, tingles. But in scripture, holiness usually looked like obedience with no applause. Like faithfulness in the mundane. Like risking your reputation, your comfort, even your life—because love asked.

Neuroscience tells us habits shape identity. Not just thought. Action. Ritual. Repetition. You become what you repeatedly do—even when you don't feel it.

Holiness isn't the mountaintop. It's the quiet refusal to give up in the valley.

It's showing up. Washing the dishes. Returning the call. Telling the truth.

It's letting grace shape your calendar, not just your theology.

So stop waiting to feel holy. Holiness isn't a mood. It's a muscle.

And it gets stronger every time you keep going when you don't feel a thing.

Room 45: Silence Is a Language Too

We treat silence like a pause. An absence. An in-between. But silence isn't what's left when the real thing stops. Sometimes, it *is* the real thing.

God's first language wasn't speech. It was void.

Before the Word, there was the wait. Before the "Let there be," there was the holy stillness that held it all.

We're afraid of silence because it doesn't confirm us. It doesn't react. It doesn't perform. But maybe that's the point. Maybe silence is what happens when truth is too whole to be broken into syllables.

In music, the rest defines the rhythm. In poetry, the line break says more than the sentence. In trauma work, regulated silence can heal more than a thousand explanations.

Silence doesn't mean absence. It means you've entered the space where God doesn't need to convince you anymore.

Elijah didn't hear God in the earthquake, the wind, or the fire. He heard a whisper. And even that whisper was surrounded by silence.

You want to hear God? Try not talking. Try not planning your reply. Try not needing an answer.

Just stay. Stay in the hush. Stay when it feels empty. Stay when nothing happens.

Because silence is not the end of the conversation. It's where the conversation finally begins.

Room 46: Forgiveness Isn't Fair

That's the point.

Forgiveness violates logic. It breaks the scales. It cancels the debt that justice insists should be paid. And still—it heals in ways punishment never could.

We want forgiveness to make sense. But real forgiveness doesn't balance the books. It burns them.

Forgiveness doesn't say, "It's okay." It says, "It mattered—and I'm not holding it against you anymore."

In therapeutic practice, forgiveness isn't forgetting. It's release. A release that rewires your physiology. Studies show that unforgiveness raises blood pressure, increases stress, and fractures neural resilience. Forgiveness, on the other hand, isn't weakness. It's nervous system repair.

But make no mistake: forgiveness costs. It costs the satisfaction of being right. The comfort of bitterness. The clarity of being the victim.

And that's why so few people truly do it. Because to forgive is to bury the weapon you had every right to use.

Jesus didn't die to keep score. He died to end the game.

You want to forgive? Let go of being right. Let go of the ending you deserved. Let go of the apology you never received.

Because forgiveness isn't fair. It's freedom.

And until you choose it, you're the one still serving the sentence.

Room 47: Every Idol Is a Mirror

We think idols are golden statues. False gods. Ancient mistakes. But idolatry isn't outdated—it's updated. It's us. It's the parts of ourselves we elevate, protect, and worship.

An idol is anything you use to avoid your reflection. And ironically, most of them look like you.

Your success. Your intelligence. Your curated spirituality. Your victimhood. Your control. These aren't just habits—they're altars. Built to keep you from facing what's fragile underneath.

In biblical terms, idols replace God. But in psychological terms, idols replace reality. They protect the ego. They buffer the truth. They let you pretend just a little longer.

Carl Jung warned that whatever you repress becomes a god. The more you deny your shadow, the more power it gains. That's how idols work—they're what you give your life to, so you don't have to give your life up.

And we don't smash them because we've stopped worshiping. We smash them because we want to see clearly.

Because behind every idol is a mirror. And behind every mirror is the fear that we're not enough without something to admire.

God doesn't ask for performance. He asks for surrender.

And the idol only falls when you stop looking at it and start asking why you needed it in the first place.

Room 48: Repentance Isn't Remorse

We've confused repentance with guilt. With shame. With groveling. But repentance isn't about feeling bad. It's about choosing different.

You can cry and not change. You can kneel and stay bitter. You can confess and still cling to the same lie. Repentance is not about emotion. It's about movement.

In Hebrew, the word is *teshuvah*—to return. Not to innocence. To alignment.

Repentance is the act of coming back to yourself. To the version of you that never needed the performance. To the clarity you buried under excuses. To the voice of God you silenced so you could keep your coping mechanism intact.

True repentance doesn't perform. It turns.

It's the decision to burn the script. To break the loop. To stop rehearsing what broke you and start writing what heals.

And it's not a moment. It's a rhythm. It's daily. Sometimes hourly. The conscious rejection of the story you used to survive but can't use to live.

Repentance is not about proving your sorrow. It's about proving your surrender.

And the proof is in the pivot. Not in the apology.

Room 49: The Sacred Refuses to Be Efficient

Efficiency is the religion of modern life. Faster. Cheaper. Smarter. Get more done with less. But the sacred doesn't hurry. The sacred meanders.

Creation didn't happen in a second. It unfolded in rhythm. Breath by breath. The divine doesn't sprint—it lingers. It waits. It returns.

We want instant healing, instant answers, instant transformation. But real growth moves like roots—underground, unseen, and slow.

We treat time like an enemy. God treats it like a canvas.

In therapy, in relationships, in prayer—nothing sacred ever happens on schedule. The breakthroughs show up late. The clarity arrives in detour. The presence comes not when we demand it, but when we finally stop demanding.

Efficiency asks, "What's the fastest way?" The sacred asks, "What's the truest?"

There's a reason Jesus walked everywhere. There's a reason silence takes time. There's a reason grace feels inefficient—because it refuses to measure worth by output.

The sacred will always be inefficient. Because it's not trying to produce. It's trying to *restore*.

And restoration never rushes.

Room 50: Redemption Is a Repeating Pattern

Redemption isn't linear. It doesn't follow a five-step plan. It doesn't climax in a perfect testimony. It's messier. Slower. A pattern that loops and returns—each time deeper, more honest, more undone.

The sacred spiral. Fall. Wake. Run. Return. Break. Rebuild. Repeat.

You don't get redeemed once. You get remade again and again— each time shedding a little more armor. Each time trusting a little faster. Each time coming home with fewer lies.

Scripture is full of returns. Jacob back to Esau. Israel back to the land. Peter back to the fire. Paul back to the people he once persecuted. Redemption isn't a finish line. It's a rhythm.

In neurobiology, the brain doesn't change through insight alone—it changes through repeated pattern disruption. Through consistent, rewired choice. Redemption is not the moment you see clearly. It's the moment you act differently.

And then the next moment. And the next.

That's why grace is designed to outlast your worst cycles. Because God knew you'd come back needing more. Not just once. But always.

Redemption is not the end of the story. It's the structure underneath every chapter.

You don't get saved and done. You get saved and started.

Room 51: Not Every Demon Comes to Kill You

Some come to clarify.

We've painted all darkness as evil. Every fear as enemy. Every ache as an invasion. But not every demon is there to destroy you. Some come to expose the lie you've been worshiping.

The desert doesn't just strip you down. It shows you what you clung to that never loved you.

Jesus was led into the wilderness—not by the devil, but by the Spirit. The confrontation was the point. The temptation was the theater for truth. You don't really know what you believe until the opposite whispers back with logic.

Carl Jung didn't believe in casting out the shadow. He believed in integrating it. Because until you befriend the parts of you that scare you, they will run your life in secret.

Demons don't always roar. Sometimes they echo. They echo your doubt, your disappointment, your buried shame. Not to annihilate you. To ask you: *Is this still yours?*

The scariest voices aren't from hell. They're the ones you inherited and never questioned.

The point of the wrestling match isn't to win. It's to walk away limping—but honest.

So no, not every demon comes to kill you. Some come to hand you the knife. And ask if you're still willing to live like this.

Room 52: Holiness Without Hunger Is Performance

You can fake reverence. You can mimic awe. But without hunger—without that gut-level ache for what's real—holiness becomes costume. Rote. Safe.

God isn't moved by polish. He's drawn to appetite.

The Psalms don't hide this. "My soul thirsts… my flesh faints." Not polite language. Desperate. Physical. Undignified. That's the liturgy heaven listens for.

Religious culture rewards performance. Sharp theology. Clean testimonies. Behavior that photographs well. But scripture tells a different story.

Jacob wrestled. Job screamed. David danced indecently.

These weren't tidy men. They were hungry. And holiness followed their hunger—not their image.

In neuroscience, desire fuels attention. What you long for shapes your perception. Hunger rewires the brain. Not just for food, but for truth. And a heart that doesn't ache, doesn't seek.

If your faith never hungers, it's not alive. It's curated.

God doesn't need your discipline. He wants your desperation.

Because the sacred isn't found by those who know where to look. It's found by those who can't stand not finding it.

So bring your hunger. Let it wreck your composure. That's where holiness begins.

Room 53: You Can't Be Found If You're Not Willing to Be Lost

We want transformation without disorientation. Change without confusion. Awakening without the ache of uncertainty. But resurrection doesn't happen in a classroom. It happens in the dark.

You can't be found unless you first allow yourself to be lost.

Lost doesn't mean damned. It means dislocated. Disrupted. Dislodged from the story that no longer fits but you're too afraid to stop telling.

Abraham left without a map. Moses wandered for forty years. Jesus disappeared for three days.

The pattern is clear: God often hides you before He reveals you.

In psychology, identity deconstruction precedes reintegration. You can't build a new sense of self on top of the old one—you have to let the old one fall apart. Spiritually, this feels like exile. But it's actually homecoming.

Most people don't change because they're too afraid to be in-between. But the sacred is always in the in-between.

The lost place is where you drop your armor. The lost place is where the false gods go silent. The lost place is where the voice of God sounds like your own breath saying, "Keep going."

You don't find yourself by standing still. You find yourself by wandering far enough that only what's real follows.

So if you're lost—good. It means you're not pretending anymore.

And if you stay honest in the dark long enough, you will be found.

Room 54: The Voice of God Sounds Like Your Own Regret

Not because God is guilt. But because regret is the echo of truth you weren't ready to face in real time.

We think God speaks through thunder. Through certainty. Through joy. But often, He speaks through the ache you keep trying to ignore.

The conversation you never finished. The promise you never kept. The moment you knew better—but stayed silent.

Regret is not condemnation. It's invitation.

Neuroscience says we replay regret because the brain wants to rewrite the story. But the soul doesn't want a rewrite. It wants reckoning. It wants you to *own it*—not to dwell, but to decide.

God doesn't weaponize regret. He waits in it.

In the story of Peter, the rooster's crow wasn't just a reminder. It was a doorway. And when Peter wept, he didn't collapse—he cracked open.

The voice of God isn't always guidance. Sometimes it's grief.

Not because He needs you to suffer. But because He knows that on the other side of regret is resolve.

You think God only speaks through comfort? Then you haven't listened closely to your regret.

It's not the end of the story. It's the moment you decide to write the next one differently.

Room 55: Awe Will Break Your Theology

You can study God until your books bleed. Memorize doctrines. Recite creeds. Build a system that fits in your back pocket. But the moment awe hits—you'll drop it all.

Awe doesn't respect structure. It breaks the frame.

It arrives unannounced: in the breath you forgot you were holding, in the sunset that steals your language, in the moment you realize the infinite isn't an idea but an intimacy.

Theology tries to define God. Awe reminds you He can't be.

Scientists call it the Overview Effect—what astronauts experience when they see Earth from orbit. Borders dissolve. Ego shatters. Perspective collapses. It's not knowledge. It's encounter.

The mystics knew: the closer you get to the divine, the more your definitions die. Not because they were wrong. But because they were too small.

Awe doesn't argue. It undoes.

It doesn't explain. It exposes.

And when it comes—whether in birth, death, heartbreak, or silence—you'll find yourself whispering the one honest theology left:

"I don't know. But I'm here."

And maybe that's all God ever wanted. Not your certainty. Just your surrender.

Room 56: Even Heaven Has Scar Tissue

We imagine heaven as untouched. Polished. Pure. Stainless. But if the risen Christ still carried His wounds, then maybe eternity doesn't erase the pain—it honors it.

Glory doesn't mean the scars are gone. It means they're finally seen.

Resurrection isn't perfection. It's wholeness.

And wholeness doesn't come from never breaking. It comes from being broken and still choosing to walk through the door.

We've taught that salvation fixes everything. That faith scrubs the past. That healing means forgetting. But the body remembers. The soul remembers. And maybe that's not a flaw. Maybe it's the proof.

In trauma recovery, healing doesn't mean erasure. It means integration. The wound becomes part of the narrative—not the end, but the hinge. The place where things changed.

The sacred is not stainless. It's storied.

Jesus didn't hide His scars. He showed them. Not as weakness, but as witness.

So if you're still carrying marks, good. It means you lived through it. It means you didn't numb or vanish or lie.

It means heaven, if it's real, has room for history. Even the kind that hurt.

Even heaven has scar tissue.

Room 57: You're Still Sacred After the Collapse

We talk about identity like it's solid. Like it survives fire. But most people don't find out who they are until the structure falls.

Not the job loss. Not the divorce. Not the diagnosis. The moment after. When the applause stops. When the plan dies. When you're standing in the ashes wondering what still breathes.

That's when you learn what's sacred isn't what survived. It's *you*.

We confuse titles with truth. But God has always used rubble as revelation. Moses didn't hear the call in Pharaoh's court. He heard it on the run. Paul didn't write scripture until he was struck blind. Resurrection doesn't happen in sanctuaries. It happens in tombs.

In neuroscience, the brain resists disruption. But post-traumatic growth is real. Sometimes collapse clears the ground for something more honest.

And God never loved your résumé. He loved your breath.

The sacred isn't in your status. It's in your staying power.

If it all fell apart—good. Now the false can stop pretending. Now the soul can speak without a script.

You're still sacred after the collapse. Not because of what you kept. But because of what you finally let go.

Room 58: God Doesn't Need Your Victory

We keep offering God our wins. Our breakthroughs. Our success stories with a bow on top. But what if that's not what moves Him? What if He's not interested in the script we perfected, but the page we tore out?

The God of scripture never asked for trophies. He asked for truth.

David wrote psalms in caves. Jonah prayed from the belly. The thief on the cross didn't have time to prove anything—he just asked.

Victory makes a great testimony. But surrender makes a real altar.

In performance culture, we're trained to showcase our highlight reel. But the soul grows in the unseen scenes. The silence. The loss. The version of you that showed up anyway.

God isn't after your image management. He's after your presence.

And the irony? Victory is most dangerous when it convinces you that you're finished. That you've arrived. But God rarely uses the triumphant. He uses the open.

So stop dressing your pain up as a lesson. Stop sanitizing your wounds. God doesn't need your victory. He wants what's real.

Bring the mess. Bring the question. Bring the moment you wanted to quit—but didn't.

That's the offering He never refuses.

Room 59: There's No Such Thing as Someone Else's Liberation

We like to think freedom is personal. That as long as *we're* healed, *we're* whole, *we're* saved—that's enough. But real liberation doesn't work like that. It's collective. Or it isn't real at all.

If your peace costs someone else their voice, it's not peace. It's privilege in disguise.

Jesus didn't just free the individual. He disrupted systems. He elevated the silenced. He touched the untouchable—not just to heal, but to dismantle the boundaries that said they didn't belong.

Liberation isn't about escape. It's about return. To the ones still trapped. Still crushed. Still waiting for someone to kick the door open and say, "You too."

Audre Lorde said, "I am not free while any woman is unfree." Paul wrote, "If one suffers, all suffer." Even heaven, if it exists, is meaningless if it's not big enough to include the ones we'd rather leave out.

Liberation is inconvenient. It'll cost you comfort. It'll call out your complicity. It'll ask if the gospel you're preaching works for the person on the bottom rung—or if it only works for you.

Because freedom that ends with you was never freedom at all.

Room 60: Holiness That Doesn't Touch Your Politics Isn't Holy

We've separated the soul from the system. Treated holiness like a private emotion. A feeling you get during worship. A glow you wear in prayer.

But if your holiness doesn't affect your politics— it's performance.

Holiness is not about retreating from the world. It's about reshaping how you move through it.

Jesus wasn't crucified for being spiritual. He was executed for being dangerous—to empire, to injustice, to every theology that protected power.

Holiness is not clean hands. It's dirty ones, reaching for the ones the system forgets.

If you say you love your neighbor but vote to cage them, deport them, displace them, disenfranchise them—your holiness is hollow.

Micah said to do justice, love mercy, walk humbly. Not to feel spiritual, but to *live differently*.

In sociology, values are only values when they cost you something. Otherwise, they're preferences. And holy people don't live by preference. They live by conviction.

If your faith makes you nicer in church but numb in public, it's not faith. It's branding.

Because holiness that only shows up in private isn't holiness. It's a costume.

And the sacred was never meant to stay on the mountain. It's meant to walk straight into the city—and refuse to leave it as it is.

Room 61: The Spirit Moves Where the System Can't

The Spirit was never meant to be domesticated. Not by doctrine. Not by denomination. Not by the liturgies we polish or the power structures we protect.

The Spirit moves wild. And wild doesn't ask for permission.

In Acts, the Spirit didn't descend in silence. It showed up in wind and flame. It confused the categories. It crossed language, nation, gender, and law.

And the system didn't know what to do with that. So it tried to tame it.

We do the same. We build walls around the wind. We draft statements of faith to contain a force that burns down every neat theology we use to feel safe.

But the Spirit doesn't need our permission. It doesn't obey our chain of command. It moves where hearts break open. Where lies are exposed. Where systems get flipped and the margins get moved to the center.

In systems theory, every structure resists disruption. But the Spirit *is* disruption. The sacred interruption. The divine sabotage.

You want to know where the Spirit is moving? Look where the comfortable are squirming. Look where the powerful are panicking. Look where the silenced are finally singing.

The Spirit moves where the system can't. Not to destroy it. But to remind it what freedom feels like.

Room 62: Faith That Never Risks Is Just Ritual

If your faith never costs you anything, it's not faith. It's habit.

We confuse routine with conviction. We equate comfort with obedience. But faith—real faith—moves. It leaps. It lets go without knowing where the ground is.

Abraham left everything. Esther risked her life. Jesus didn't just teach faith. He walked into death with it.

Faith isn't a doctrine you recite. It's a fire that pushes you into places you would never choose without it.

In behavioral science, risk creates engagement. The brain activates differently when the outcome isn't guaranteed. Faith functions the same—it doesn't thrive in certainty. It thrives in surrender.

But we've built a culture where faith is rehearsed, not risked. Where it's more about saying the right things than stepping into the terrifying unknown.

We say we trust God. But we rarely bet anything on it.

Faith that never risks is just ritual. And ritual without risk becomes religion without relevance.

So ask yourself: When was the last time your faith made your knees shake? When was the last time it asked more of you than comfort could offer?

Because if it hasn't hurt yet, it probably hasn't started yet.

Room 63: The Devil Wears Doctrine

Not because truth is evil. But because lies wrapped in scripture are the most seductive of all.

The devil doesn't tempt you with rebellion. He tempts you with certainty.

He twists the holy into armor. Turns verses into weapons. Makes you so convinced of your own righteousness that you stop hearing God entirely.

The serpent didn't lie in Eden. He distorted. He quoted God almost exactly. Just enough truth to sell the death underneath.

That's how evil works. Not through chaos. Through counterfeit.

We forget that when Jesus was tempted, the devil used scripture. Verbatim.

And Jesus didn't argue. He redirected. Because the Word isn't just ink—it's presence. And presence can't be weaponized without breaking.

In psychology, the most dangerous beliefs are the ones that validate your ego. Doctrine is no different. If your theology always makes you the good guy, you're not reading the gospel. You're rewriting it.

The devil doesn't need to make you wicked. He just needs to make you certain.

So test every truth. Especially the ones that flatter you. Especially the ones that justify your superiority.

Because sometimes the most dangerous lie is the one you preach in God's name.

And sometimes, the devil wears doctrine.

Room 64: Grace That Doesn't Cost You Power Isn't Grace

We've tamed grace. We've made it polite. Passive. An emotional balm with no teeth. But real grace is disruptive. It levels hierarchies. It doesn't just forgive—it rearranges who gets to speak, who gets to lead, who gets to belong.

Grace without power shift is just pity. And pity is a counterfeit gospel.

The prodigal son didn't just get a robe. He got a place at the table. And that means the older brother had to sit next to someone he thought disqualified.

That's what grace does. It forces a reckoning.

In liberation theology, grace isn't abstract. It's material. It changes structures, not just hearts. Because if grace doesn't reach the oppressed in tangible ways, it's not grace—it's sentiment.

Power doesn't surrender easily. So we reinvent grace as something personal. Private. But Jesus never kept grace small. He fed crowds. He freed women. He touched untouchables. His grace got loud. And it got Him killed.

So if your version of grace doesn't cost you comfort, advantage, or status— it's probably not grace.

Grace costs. It costs your right to be first. It costs your certainty about who belongs. It costs the illusion that your place is secure because you earned it.

The gospel was never about inclusion without disruption. It was always about the table being rebuilt.

And grace flips it—every time.

Room 65: Holiness Without Grief Is Hollow

We act like holiness is brightness. Light. Clean. Triumphant. But real holiness walks with a limp. It mourns. Because if it doesn't carry grief, it's not grounded—it's just performance.

Grief is what roots you to the world you're trying to heal.

You don't become holy by escaping pain. You become holy by letting it change you.

Jesus wept. He didn't explain death away. He stood in it. Let it move through Him. And then He did something miraculous—but not before honoring the ache.

The saints didn't float above sorrow. They held it. Named it. Let it break them open instead of hardening them shut.

In trauma-informed therapy, grief is part of integration. Not something to fix, but something to face. The only way out of suffering is through it—and grief is the honest road.

Holiness that denies grief is brittle. It cracks under reality.

But holiness that grieves? That's strength. That's presence. That's the kind of sacred that doesn't flinch when the world falls apart.

You want to be holy? Start by letting yourself mourn. Mourn what hurt. Mourn who left. Mourn what didn't become.

And let that mourning turn you into someone who loves wider. Because holiness without grief is hollow. And love that hasn't wept isn't ready to stay.

Room 66: Your Theology Ends Where Your Neighbor Bleeds

The real test of what you believe isn't your statement of faith. It's what you do when someone suffers—and it doesn't fit your framework.

Do you rush to explain? Do you quote a verse? Do you retreat into certainty because their pain threatens your system?

Your theology doesn't matter until it bleeds. Until it bends. Until it breaks open enough to hold someone else's crisis.

Jesus never responded to suffering with a lecture. He responded with presence. He touched. He sat. He fed. He healed. And only *then* did He speak.

If your theology can't make room for questions without answers—it's not holy. It's just fragile.

Good theology stretches. Bad theology stiffens.

In social psychology, cognitive rigidity is a sign of fear, not faith. When your beliefs require everything to fit neatly, you're no longer worshiping God—you're worshiping control.

So here's the rule: If your theology can't make room for your neighbor's trauma, your theology ends there. Not because God is limited. But because you are.

Truth that cannot love is not truth. It's a mask.

And God doesn't hide behind masks. He tears them.

Room 67: The Sacred Doesn't Rush Grief

We want grief to be linear. Orderly. Predictable. Done in stages, on schedule, preferably quiet.

But sacred grief doesn't move like that. It spirals. It reopens. It shows up uninvited years later when a smell, a sound, or a season calls it back.

And God doesn't rush it. He sits in it.

Jesus wept not because He lacked hope—but because love doesn't bypass pain. Even when resurrection is coming.

In trauma studies, unprocessed grief gets trapped. It surfaces later as illness, rage, or apathy. The soul demands to be heard, even if it has to scream.

The sacred honors that scream. It doesn't edit it. It doesn't spiritualize it. It listens.

Most religion wants to tidy grief into testimony. But real holiness knows: the wound is still holy before it heals.

If your theology can't wait with someone in the dark, it's not theology. It's abandonment in sacred clothing.

The sacred doesn't rush grief. It holds the silence. It bears witness. It stays.

And sometimes, that's the holiest thing you can do.

Room 68: Holiness Begins Where You Break Your Silence

Most people don't hide sin. They hide suffering.

They hide the secret bruise of disappointment. The buried scream of unmet expectations. The chronic ache of spiritual hunger in a room full of people pretending to be full.

Holiness doesn't begin with behavior. It begins with brutal honesty.

The moment you stop smiling through your fracture. The moment you say, "I'm not okay"—not as a confession, but as a declaration of presence.

Silence is where shame survives. But holiness? It's allergic to secrets.

The first thing God did in Genesis was speak. Light came from language. Truth from utterance.

And your healing won't begin until your voice returns.

In therapy, naming trauma reduces its grip. Naming isn't just catharsis—it's reclamation. It's dragging the thing out of the dark and putting it where it can't grow unchecked.

The sacred doesn't demand perfection. It demands exposure.

You don't become holy by hiding your hurt. You become holy by naming it so clearly, it loses its power to isolate you.

So stop whispering. Say it out loud. Say it before it's polished. Say it before it's safe.

Because holiness begins where you finally decide to stop lying to survive.

Room 69: Grace Will Make You Weep for People You Once Judged

Not because you've gone soft. But because your heart finally broke open wide enough to hold them.

Real grace doesn't just forgive—it rewires. It rewrites your instincts. Your reactions. Your hierarchy of who deserves compassion.

You used to see their behavior. Now you see their bruises. You used to roll your eyes. Now you drop your guard.

That's what grace does. It wrecks your moral superiority. It dismantles the illusion that you ever earned anything.

In social neuroscience, empathy is trainable. Not taught—*caught*. The more you're shown mercy, the more your brain maps mercy into your response system. Grace isn't a belief. It's a neurological shift.

Jesus didn't draw lines around sinners. He ate with them. Touched them. Wept for them.

And when you start walking like Him, your tears will betray you. You'll cry in rooms you used to judge. You'll embrace people you used to write off. You'll pray for the ones you used to fear.

Grace does that. It humiliates your ego—and raises your empathy.

So if you've wept lately—not for yourself, but for someone you thought didn't deserve it—

That's not weakness. That's the Spirit.

And that's where the real healing starts.

Room 70: Healing Doesn't Always Look Like Progress

Sometimes healing looks like sleeping twelve hours. Like saying no to the invitation. Like canceling the plan. Like crying for no clear reason and not needing to justify it.

We've confused healing with hustle. With always getting better. With a chart that climbs steadily upward. But real healing? It loops. It limps. It lingers.

And God doesn't rush you. He meets you in the stall.

The woman who touched Jesus's robe didn't give a speech. She reached. That was enough.

In psychology, recovery is non-linear. Setbacks are not failure—they're data. Signals. Your body asking for more tenderness than before.

Healing doesn't always look brave. Sometimes it looks like hiding. Like resting. Like asking someone else to speak when your voice is gone.

And holiness doesn't require momentum. It requires presence.

Jesus never told the hemorrhaging woman to hurry. He stopped the whole crowd for her pause.

So if today's healing doesn't look like victory, don't apologize. Don't edit. Don't measure it by someone else's metric.

Sometimes the holiest thing you can do is stay in bed tell the truth and trust that the sacred moves even when you don't.

Room 71: The Sacred Is Not a Secret Club

We've made access to God conditional. Dress this way. Believe this. Belong here. Don't question too much. Don't feel too deeply. Don't deviate.

But the sacred was never meant to be gated. It's not a club. It's a current—flowing everywhere, touching everyone, especially the ones who were told they don't qualify.

Jesus didn't build walls. He broke them.

He talked to the Samaritan woman. He healed the Roman soldier's servant. He dined with tax collectors. He let women sit at His feet. He said, "Let the children come."

We've turned holiness into exclusivity. But sacredness isn't about separation. It's about saturation.

In anthropology, liminality is the space between what was and what's becoming. The sacred often lives here—in the blurry, the rejected, the undefined. That's where God shows up.

And if your spirituality only makes space for people who already think like you, vote like you, pray like you— it's not spirituality. It's tribalism in religious clothing.

You don't guard sacred ground. You kneel on it.

And if someone reaches for God with trembling hands and messy theology and a life that doesn't fit your system—

Make room. Or get out of the way.

Because the sacred doesn't belong to you. It never did.

Room 72: Salvation Is Not an Escape Plan

We've treated salvation like a ticket. Punch it. Pocket it. Wait for heaven. But that's not rescue—it's avoidance. It's turning eternity into insurance.

Salvation isn't about exit. It's about embodiment.

Jesus didn't say, "Go to heaven." He said, "Follow me." Not up. But through. Through injustice. Through conflict. Through community. Through death, even.

We keep looking for rescue from the world. God keeps offering redemption within it.

In Hebrew thought, salvation (*yeshuah*) means spaciousness. Liberation into a wider place. It's not just what you're saved *from*—it's what you're saved *for*.

To be fully here. Fully human. Fully present.

We want to disappear. God wants to dwell.

That's why Jesus wept. Why He touched lepers. Why He bled. Because salvation is not abstract. It's incarnate. It shows up with skin on, in the dirt, with the hungry and the haunted and the ones who can't wait for heaven because they're barely surviving today.

So if your gospel skips suffering, skips systems, skips solidarity— it's not salvation. It's spiritual bypassing.

You don't get saved to escape. You get saved to engage. To walk back into the fire you came from and pull someone else out.

Room 73: God Won't Compete With Your Idols

God isn't insecure. But He is uncompromising.

Not because He needs attention, but because your idols are killing you slowly—and He knows it.

You keep praying for clarity, but clinging to control. Keep asking for peace, but worshiping productivity. Keep quoting scripture, but bowing to image, influence, and applause.

God won't shout over what you keep turning up. He waits. And waits. And waits—until the noise doesn't work anymore.

In the Old Testament, God didn't just condemn idols—He called them worthless. Not to shame, but to warn: "They can't hold you. They can't speak. They can't save."

Modern idols aren't statues. They're stories you refuse to let die.

In neuroscience, the brain attaches to reward systems—even false ones. If it numbs the ache, even briefly, it earns loyalty. But addiction is not affection. And God doesn't want your addiction. He wants your *allegiance*.

So don't be surprised when the idol collapses. When the job falls through. When the platform crumbles. When the spotlight turns and leaves you alone with your echo.

That's not punishment. That's mercy.

Because God won't compete with your idols. He'll wait for them to fail. So you'll finally remember what real love feels like.

Room 74: You Can't Fast Your Way Out of Being Human

We keep using spiritual practices to escape ourselves. Fasting to outrun hunger. Prayer to drown desire. Worship to avoid the weight of our own bodies.

But you can't fast your way out of being human.

Jesus fasted—but not to become less human. He did it to face what it means to be human without shortcuts.

The flesh isn't the enemy. It's the location.

We've mistaken asceticism for holiness. But starving your body doesn't feed your soul. And killing desire doesn't make you divine—it makes you dishonest.

Real sanctity doesn't bypass hunger. It brings it to the table.

In trauma work, dissociation happens when we disconnect from the body to survive. But healing only happens when we come back to it. Slowly. Tenderly. Truthfully.

You don't get holy by escaping your body. You get holy by coming home to it.

Touching the hunger. Naming the ache. Telling the truth about how tired you are.

God didn't become spirit. He became flesh.

So if your spiritual life keeps pulling you out of your body— maybe it's not spirit you're following. Maybe it's shame in disguise.

You can't fast your way out of being human. You can only learn to bless it.

Room 75: The God Who Leaves the Ninety-Nine

We quote the parable like it's sweet. Like it's sentimental. But the math is reckless. One out of ninety-nine? That's not strategy. That's scandal.

And that's the point.

God doesn't operate by risk management. He doesn't guard the flock and hope the missing one finds their way back. He goes.

Not because the one is more valuable. But because love refuses to let absence be the final word.

In human systems, we favor the majority. We protect the stable. We write off what wanders.

But the sacred doesn't. It chases. It leaves safety. It risks loss for love.

In trauma-informed psychology, rupture followed by repair builds resilience. The healing is not in never breaking—it's in the pursuit after the break.

This is the God who leaves the ninety-nine. Who breaks the rules of efficiency. Who rewrites what fairness looks like.

Because sometimes holiness is not staying put. It's running after the lost thing with wild, unapologetic grace.

And if you've ever felt like the one who wandered too far— this is your proof: God didn't wait for you to come home. He came after you.

Room 76: Holiness Has a Body Count

We talk about holiness like it's polite. Like it's a virtue that fits inside a sermon or a song. But real holiness disrupts. It dismantles. It threatens the empire enough to get you killed.

Ask the prophets. Ask the martyrs. Ask Jesus.

Holiness doesn't blend in. It offends. It flips tables. It breaks systems that preserve the illusion of order at the cost of truth.

In every era, real holiness makes power flinch. It exposes the lie behind the throne. It names what everyone benefits from ignoring.

And power always responds the same way: Silence it. Crucify it. Explain it away.

In liberation theology, holiness is not an interior condition. It's an embodied resistance. A refusal to separate love from justice, soul from system, prayer from protest.

Holiness got Jesus killed. Not because He was divine. But because He wouldn't stop healing on the wrong day. Feeding the wrong people. Touching what was untouchable.

If your holiness doesn't cost you comfort, If it doesn't call out injustice, If it's only practiced in safe places— it's not holiness. It's theater.

Because holiness, real holiness, always has a body count. And still it keeps walking into danger, unafraid to bleed for what's sacred.

Room 77: The Sacred Stutters

Not every holy word is smooth. Not every sacred voice is strong. Sometimes the truest thing comes out broken, halting, ashamed to be heard.

And God listens anyway.

We think power comes in polish. But scripture is full of the stammering. Moses begged not to speak. Jeremiah was too young. Paul's letters were awkward. Even Jesus stayed silent before Pilate.

The sacred doesn't need eloquence. It needs honesty.

In speech therapy, they say stuttering isn't a flaw in thought. It's a fracture in the bridge between the soul and the sound. And sometimes the most profound truths arrive unannounced, wrapped in imperfection.

We've built pulpits for the slick. Platforms for the practiced. But the prophets? They cried. They hesitated. They fell apart mid-sentence.

Because sacredness isn't in the performance. It's in the permission to speak anyway.

God doesn't wait for clarity. He moves at the sound of trembling.

If your voice shakes, let it. If you forget your lines, improvise. If you can't find the words, groan.

The Spirit translates. The heavens interpret. And holiness makes room for every stutter that dares to rise from a real place.

Because the sacred doesn't shout. It stutters. And still, it changes everything.

Room 78: Your Shadow Prays Too

We pretend our darkness disappears when we kneel. That prayer is a light switch. That when we speak to God, only the best of us is allowed in the room.

But your shadow kneels beside you. And God hears that voice too.

The anger you won't name. The envy you hide. The addiction you justify. The pride disguised as discipline.

You think God only meets your better angels? He meets the parts you exiled. The parts you lied about. The parts you hoped to bury in a verse.

Carl Jung said the shadow is the "thing a person has no wish to be." But the Spirit doesn't avoid it. The Spirit integrates.

Because real transformation doesn't come from suppression. It comes from surrender.

You don't get holy by pretending you're light. You get holy by letting the dark speak— by letting it confess, not just what it's done, but what it longs for.

The most honest prayers you'll ever pray might be the ones you're too ashamed to say out loud.

Pray them anyway. Let the shadow kneel. Let the whole of you be seen.

Because God doesn't flinch at your darkness. He brought a table big enough for it.

And your shadow prays too.

Room 79: Not All Fire Is From God

We've been taught that fire means presence. That every blaze is holy. That if it burns, it must be sacred.

But not all fire is from God. Some flames are forged from ego. From envy dressed as zeal. From control wrapped in charisma.

We've mistaken heat for light.

Elijah called down fire. But so did the false prophets. And when James and John wanted to torch a village, Jesus rebuked them—not because they lacked power, but because they misunderstood the purpose.

In neuroscience, emotional arousal mimics conviction. But fire without discernment is just destruction with branding.

Passion is easy. Holiness is harder.

One consumes. The other refines.

You want to know if the fire is from God? Check what's left when it's over.

If it leaves only ash and applause, it wasn't holy. If it leaves truth, tenderness, and a clearer path to love—it was.

God's fire doesn't need spectacle. It needs surrender.

Because the Spirit doesn't burn to be seen. It burns to purify. To illuminate. To guide.

Not all fire is from God. So stop chasing heat. Start seeking light.

Room 80: Some Doors Only Open from the Inside

You can't drag someone into healing. You can't pry their fists open. You can't break a wall that was built to survive.

Some doors only open from the inside.

Love doesn't kick down defenses. It waits. It knocks. It leaves space for the miracle of surrender.

Jesus stood at the door and knocked. He didn't barge in. Because forced salvation isn't salvation. It's colonization.

In trauma recovery, safety precedes transformation. No one can heal while being coerced. Trust must choose to open. And it won't if fear is still sitting in the hallway.

We confuse urgency with care. But urgency often centers our discomfort with their timeline.

Love stays. But it doesn't shove.

So if they're not ready—bless them anyway. If they're still closed— respect the boundary. If you're tempted to rescue—check whether it's love or ego.

Because God never kicks in doors. He stands and knocks. And the holiest things grow slowly in locked rooms, until the heart decides it's safe enough to say yes.

Room 81: The Altar Is Not at the Front of the Room

We've been trained to think the altar is a place. A raised platform. A stage. A set of steps bathed in lights and music.

But the real altar? It's wherever you decide to lay something down.

Not performatively. Not for applause. But quietly. Secretly. Sometimes desperately.

In scripture, altars were built in wildernesses. Not temples. They marked the moment something ended —and something else had to begin.

You carry the tools. Your hands. Your confession. Your willingness to let go of what no longer brings life.

In therapeutic spaces, breakthroughs often happen off-script— in a sigh, a pause, a sentence spoken too softly to perform. That's an altar. Not because it's loud, but because it's real.

You don't need a building. You need honesty.

The altar is not up front. It's wherever the false finally dies. It's wherever your ego kneels. It's wherever you stop praying with pretense and start speaking like someone who has nothing left to protect.

So build one. Right where you are. Out of your fear. Out of your fatigue. Out of your trembling voice that finally says: "I'm done pretending."

That's the altar. That's where everything begins again.

Room 82: God Is Not in the Answer

We keep asking questions like they're keys. Like if we say it right, God will unlock the silence. But what if the silence *is* the answer?

What if the answer is the asking? What if the presence comes not in what you learn, but in what you endure?

Job never got an explanation. He got a whirlwind. A presence too large for language, too wild for logic. And somehow—it was enough.

We've made an idol out of clarity. Out of systematized theology. Out of clean diagrams of salvation and sin.

But God doesn't fit into flowcharts. He fits into mystery.

In mysticism, God is not a solution. He's a saturation. A being-with. Not the answer, but the awareness you're not alone in the ache.

Cognitive science confirms this: The brain craves closure—but the soul doesn't. The soul grows through tension. Through contradiction. Through sitting with what cannot be solved.

So ask. Cry. Pound the table. But stop demanding a God who explains Himself. Start trusting a God who stays when nothing makes sense.

Because the answer was never the point. The point was presence.

And He is here. Even now. Especially now.

Room 83: Some Truth Only Arrives After the Breakdown

We want to understand while everything's still intact. While the house is standing. While the reputation is spotless. While we still feel in control.

But some truths don't knock. They collapse the ceiling.

You don't get them from books. You get them from breaking. From sitting in the debris long enough to realize that the rubble isn't the end—it's the beginning of what finally matters.

Paul didn't write epistles until prison. Moses didn't meet God until exile. Mary didn't carry Christ until she risked shame.

The sacred doesn't arrive on schedule. It arrives in aftermath.

In psychology, cognitive restructuring often follows trauma—not because pain teaches, but because pain strips away what never worked in the first place.

We don't change when we're comfortable. We change when the scaffolding fails.

That's where real truth shows up. Not to punish. To rebuild.

So if you're sitting in the ruins, if the narrative just fell apart, if the mask cracked and nothing makes sense anymore—

wait. Something holy is waking up beneath the wreckage.

Some truth only arrives after the breakdown.

Let it come.

Room 84: Worship That Doesn't Cost You Isn't Worship

We've made worship easy. A playlist. A vibe. A performance. But worship was never meant to be convenient. It was always meant to be costly.

David said, "I will not offer to the Lord that which costs me nothing." Because worship is not applause. It's sacrifice.

Not a song. A surrender.

In scripture, worship meant building altars. Dragging stones. Splitting wood. Carrying animals. Sweat, blood, fire. Not comfort. Consecration.

And in your life, real worship might mean laying down your certainty. Your reputation. Your narrative. Your pride.

In neuroscience, pattern interruption creates neuroplastic change. Worship that costs something reshapes the brain—it breaks routine, creates surrender, awakens the deeper self.

If your worship always feels good, it probably isn't deep enough.

Because the sacred doesn't just soothe. It strips.

It pulls you into presence. Not with polish, but with pain. Not with image, but with offering.

You want to worship? Then bleed a little. Weep honestly. Put something real on the altar and walk away empty-handed.

Because worship that doesn't cost you isn't worship. It's aesthetics.

And God isn't looking for a mood. He's looking for surrender.

Room 85: You're Not Disqualified

Not by the divorce. Not by the relapse. Not by the years you lost pretending. Not by the silence you didn't break in time.

Shame says, "You blew it." Grace says, "You're still called."

We keep thinking sacredness is a straight line. That calling means consistency. That if you ever fall hard enough, God crosses your name off the list.

But God writes in permanent ink.

Moses murdered a man. David manipulated and stole. Peter denied everything. Paul was a terrorist.

And still—they built altars. They wrote psalms. They led. They loved. They limped their way into legacy.

In trauma recovery, restoration isn't about going back. It's about integrating what broke you into something truer than before.

God doesn't erase your past. He repurposes it.

So bring the failure. Bring the fall. Bring the part of you that says, "I don't belong anymore."

Because your disqualification was never God's decision. And your comeback doesn't need anyone's permission.

You're not too late. You're not too far. You're not disqualified.

You're ready.

Room 86: God Doesn't Bless Who You Pretend to Be

You can fake it. In church. In therapy. Even in prayer. You can wear the mask so long you start to forget it's there.

But God doesn't bless the version of you you invented to survive. He blesses the one underneath.

The stammering one. The jealous one. The anxious, impulsive, doubting mess that you've been trained to hide.

We keep presenting the cleaned-up self. The disciplined self. The marketable testimony. But God meets the one curled up behind the fig leaves.

The blessing only sticks when it hits real skin.

Jacob wrestled all night for it. But it wasn't until he gave his real name—*the one that meant deceiver*—that the blessing came.

In internal family systems therapy, healing begins when every part is allowed to speak. Even the parts you hate. Especially the parts you hate.

God isn't in love with your performance. He's in love with your presence.

So take off the mask. Drop the act. Let the you that still winces when you pray finally speak.

Because God doesn't bless who you pretend to be. He blesses the real you.

Even if you've never introduced yourself.

Room 87: Sacred Doesn't Mean Spectacular

We think the sacred should sparkle. That if it's real, it'll roar. Dazzle. Convince everyone at once.

But most of the holy moments? They're quiet. Unspectacular. Small enough to miss if you're waiting for fireworks.

The burning bush didn't part the sky. It flickered.

The still, small voice didn't shake mountains. It whispered.

Jesus came back from the dead and didn't appear in the temple. He made breakfast.

Sacred isn't always loud. It's often low.

In psychology, transformation happens not in climactic moments, but in micro-decisions. Tiny rewrites. Neural whispers that build a new narrative, one gentle step at a time.

And yet we keep chasing spectacle. We think if it doesn't change everything instantly, it must not be God.

But the sacred doesn't show off. It stays.

It shows up in the conversation that doesn't go viral. In the habit no one sees. In the apology that trembles through gritted teeth.

Don't miss the miracle because it wasn't dramatic. Don't walk past the burning bush because it's not burning down the forest.

Sacred doesn't mean spectacular. It means real.

And real is enough.

Room 88: Repentance That Doesn't Repair Is Just Relief

We've confused repentance with emotion. Tears. Guilt. A moment at the altar. But real repentance doesn't stop with sorrow. It builds something new.

Repentance isn't how bad you feel. It's how different you live.

Zacchaeus didn't just say sorry. He paid people back. Four times over. Because transformation demands repair.

You can't repent without returning what was taken. You can't confess while still benefiting from the harm. You can't preach grace and avoid the cost of justice.

In restorative justice, healing comes through accountability—not punishment, but presence. Naming the damage. Asking what repair looks like to the wounded, not the comfortable.

But we keep making repentance a performance. A show of remorse without responsibility.

God isn't moved by the tears if the system stays the same. God doesn't need your shame. He wants your shift.

So if your repentance ends with your comfort, if it demands nothing of you but a clean conscience, it's not repentance. It's escape.

Repentance that doesn't repair is just relief. And relief is not redemption.

Change something. Give something back. Say it to their face.

Then you'll know it's real.

Room 89: Some Walls Are Holy Until They're Not

Boundaries are sacred. They protect. They hold. They give shape to freedom. But sometimes the wall that saved you becomes the wall that cages you.

Not every wall is meant to last.

The temple veil was holy—until it tore. The law was divine—until grace rewrote it in flesh. Even Jesus broke Sabbath rules to heal, to touch, to love.

What begins as sacred can harden into a shield. And shields don't just block arrows—they block light.

In psychology, defense mechanisms form for survival. But what protected you yesterday might isolate you today.

Walls aren't wrong. But they have to breathe. They have to move when the Spirit moves.

We say, "This is how it's always been." But God says, "Behold, I do a new thing."

So ask yourself: Is this boundary a container or a cage? Is this wall protecting life—or avoiding change?

Because some walls are holy. Until they're not.

And holiness never clings to what God already walked past.

Room 90: Love That Doesn't Cost You Isn't Love

We throw the word around like it's soft. As if love is always ease, always warmth, always return. But real love? Real love bleeds.

If it never costs you, it's convenience. Not love.

Love is what you do after it stops being mutual. After the text goes unanswered. After the person forgets your birthday. After they say something that makes you question if they even saw you at all.

The cross wasn't just forgiveness. It was the price love was willing to pay—with nothing guaranteed in return.

In attachment theory, true connection requires risk. Not co-dependence. Not withdrawal. But presence—even when vulnerability feels like exposure.

Jesus didn't just love when it was safe. He loved when it was betrayal. He loved knowing the kiss would come.

You can say "I love you" a thousand times. But love doesn't prove itself in speech. It proves itself in sacrifice.

Your comfort. Your time. Your ego. Your right to be right.

So if your love costs you nothing, if it only shows up when it's returned, if it never puts something on the altar—

It's not love. It's a mirror.

And love isn't about reflection. It's about offering.

Room 91: The Sacred Isn't Afraid of Your Rage

We think anger disqualifies us. We think fury is unholy. We flinch when it rises, shove it down, or translate it into silence.

But rage is not the opposite of sacred. Sometimes it *is* the sacred—on fire.

Moses shattered tablets. Jeremiah screamed at God. Jesus flipped tables.

The sacred doesn't shrink from your fire. It meets it.

In trauma recovery, rage is often the first true voice to surface after numbness. It's not dysfunction. It's resurrection.

Anger reveals what mattered. Anger unmasks what's broken. Anger, when aimed with truth, becomes holy resistance.

We've made peace the goal. But peace without protest isn't peace. It's pacification.

So bring your anger. Bring your betrayal. Bring your holy howl.

Not to be tamed. But to be heard.

Because the sacred doesn't need you quiet. It needs you real. And rage might be the only language left when the systems built to protect you turn their backs.

God's not afraid of your rage. He lit the bush with fire. And still called it holy.

Room 92: The Bible Isn't a Weapon

We turned a library into a blade. Stripped it of context. Flattened its contradictions. Used it to dominate instead of to deliver.

But the Bible was never meant to be a weapon. It was meant to be a window.

Into grief. Into liberation. Into a God who would rather bleed than be right.

Jesus didn't quote scripture to control. He quoted it to resist. To root Himself in a deeper truth than power could twist.

If you need the Bible to win an argument, you've already missed the point.

In hermeneutics, interpretation is shaped by your lens. What you want to see, you'll find. And if what you want is domination, there are verses that will comply.

But if what you want is freedom? There's a whole gospel waiting.

The Bible is a witness. Not a weapon. It holds multitudes. Lament and praise. Contradiction and clarity. Wrestling and wonder.

So read it. But don't aim it.

Wielding the Bible to wound isn't bold. It's lazy.

The Word became flesh, not ammo. And that flesh was pierced, not protected.

Room 93: Holiness Doesn't Happen in a Vacuum

You can't get holy alone. Not really. Because holiness isn't an achievement. It's a relationship. A rhythm of presence. Of interruption. Of letting someone else's need reroute your plan.

We think spiritual growth happens in silence. But more often—it happens in traffic. In the argument. In the confession that interrupts your comfort.

God didn't design holiness as isolation. He built it into community.

Love your neighbor. Bear one another's burdens. Forgive seventy times seven.

None of that works without friction. None of that means anything in a vacuum.

In systems theory, change emerges through interaction. Selfhood is shaped not by solitude alone, but by contact. Tension. Repair.

You don't know your patience until someone tests it. You don't know your compassion until someone needs it. You don't know your holiness until it costs you something in public.

So pray. Fast. Read. But don't confuse quiet with sacred.

The sacred often shouts. In someone else's pain. In a knock on your door when you're tired. In a text you didn't expect—but can't ignore.

Because holiness doesn't happen in a vacuum. It happens in the mess. In the noise. In the decision to stay open anyway.

Room 94: Some Altars Are Built From Ash

Not everything sacred starts with beauty. Some starts with loss. With what you didn't choose. With what you couldn't save.

We think altars are made of stone. But sometimes they're made of ruin. Of the burned-out hope. The shattered plan. The pieces you gathered when the fire was done.

God doesn't just meet you in the temple. He meets you in the aftermath.

Job's altar was a broken body and unanswered questions. Hannah's was years of weeping and silence. Jesus's was a cross.

You don't need something whole to build an altar. You just need something honest.

In grief therapy, meaning doesn't erase the loss. It grows in the soil of it. Meaning is not denial—it's presence in what remains.

So bring what's left. The scorched wood. The forgotten dream. The ember of a faith you're not even sure is still burning.

Stack it. Name it. Light it again.

Because some altars are built from ash. And that doesn't make them less holy. It makes them real.

Room 95: There's No Shortcut to Resurrection

We want to skip the tomb. To go from death to dancing in a single verse. But resurrection doesn't come with a bypass. It comes with burial.

You don't rise until you've been still. Until you've been sealed in. Until everything you thought would save you has gone quiet.

Jesus didn't cheat the grave. He entered it fully. Stayed the night. Waited while the world thought it was over.

In healing, integration always follows rest. The nervous system doesn't reboot through force—it settles through surrender.

But we keep trying to rush our way back to life. We call it "faith." God calls it avoidance.

If you want resurrection, you have to let the old thing die. Completely. No pretending. No performance. No half-measures.

Let it rot. Let it be mourned. Let it become nothing.

And then—only then—watch what God does with the silence.

Because there is no shortcut to resurrection. And the stone doesn't roll away until death has done its work.

Room 96: Some Miracles Don't Fix You

We expect miracles to restore everything. To erase the limp. To undo the damage. To make it like it never happened.

But some miracles leave marks.

Lazarus came back—but he still had to die again. Paul got vision, but not immunity. Jesus rose—but kept the scars.

Some miracles don't fix you. They *carry* you.

We pray for healing and think it means wholeness. But sometimes healing means walking with the wound —and not being ruled by it.

In neurobiology, trauma never fully vanishes. It integrates. It re-threads itself into story. The miracle isn't forgetting. It's remembering—and still moving.

God's power isn't proven by erasing pain. It's proven by walking with you through it. Not above it. Not around it. Right through the middle.

So stop waiting to feel perfect before you testify. Stop waiting for the full fix. The miracle may not be your recovery. It might be your return.

To presence. To love. To the version of yourself that no longer hides.

Because some miracles don't fix you. They free you to live—with the wound—wide open.

Room 97: You Don't Have to Understand to Obey

We treat obedience like a conclusion. Something you do once everything makes sense. But in the kingdom of God, obedience often comes *before* clarity.

Abraham walked without a map. Noah built before rain had a name. Mary said yes without knowing what it would cost.

Understanding is comfortable. But it's not required.

Obedience isn't submission to certainty. It's surrender to trust.

In developmental psychology, secure attachment doesn't come from always understanding—it comes from knowing you're held even in the dark.

Faith without mystery isn't faith. It's management.

We keep waiting to feel ready. God keeps waiting for us to move.

Not because He needs us to prove anything, but because the miracle lives on the other side of our yes.

So go before you're sure. Say yes before the blueprint. Step even if your hands shake.

You don't need to understand to obey. You just need to trust the One who called you.

And when the fog clears, you'll see you were never lost. Just led.

Room 98: Blessings Sometimes Look Like Breakups

We pray for favor. We ask for open doors. But we don't expect the blessing to come as loss. As rupture. As someone walking out.

But sometimes that *is* the blessing.

Not because the pain isn't real. But because the ending was holy.

God doesn't always deliver by addition. Sometimes He rescues you through subtraction.

You didn't fail. You outgrew. You woke up. You saw what you couldn't keep making excuses for.

In behavioral psychology, detachment from toxic reinforcement is progress—even when it hurts. Freedom isn't always light at first. Sometimes it's heavy with grief.

But grief is not a curse. It's evidence you loved deeply enough to feel it end.

Abraham had to leave his home. Jesus lost followers. Paul walked away from prestige.

The blessing wasn't in what they kept. It was in who they became after letting go.

So stop calling it failure when something falls apart. Start asking what had to die for you to live.

Because blessings sometimes look like breakups. And deliverance doesn't always knock. Sometimes it walks away.

Room 99: Your Wound Knows the Way

We keep trying to lead with strength. With what we've mastered. What we've healed. What we've already made peace with.

But your power isn't in your polish. It's in your wound.

That's where compassion lives. That's where your integrity was born. That's the map you never wanted—but can now hand to someone else still lost in it.

Jesus didn't show His resume after resurrection. He showed His scars.

In narrative therapy, the most redemptive stories come not from avoidance but from integration. You don't have to conquer the pain. You have to *carry* it well.

And when you lead from your limp, you lead others out of hiding.

Because a healed person with no memory of their wound is just another judge in a choir robe. But a healed person who remembers what broke them becomes sanctuary.

Your wound knows the way. To empathy. To wisdom. To a kind of presence that can't be faked.

So don't wait to be fixed before you show up. You're not here to prove perfection. You're here to bleed honestly and say:

"I've been there. I made it. And you can too."

Room 100: God Is Still Speaking

Not in thunder. Not just in scripture. But in you.

In your breath when you thought you were done. In your dream that won't let go. In the ache that refuses to stay numb.

God didn't stop talking when the canon closed. He didn't lose His voice when the ink dried.

The Word became flesh. And flesh keeps moving.

In mysticism, divine communication is not static. It's continuous. Ongoing. Present. The sacred doesn't fossilize. It flows.

We think revelation is reserved for prophets. But what if it's happening right now? In your journal. In your therapy session. In your silence.

God speaks through joy. Through memory. Through the interruption you didn't see coming.

He speaks in your hunger. In your protest. In your prayer that sounds more like a groan than a sentence.

And if you've been waiting for a sign— this is it:

You're still here. You're still listening. That's the proof.

God is still speaking. So write it down. Say it out loud. Live like it's true.

Because it is.